THE **facebook** EFFECT

FOR LAWYERS

THE **facebook** EFFECT
FOR LAWYERS

ADVERTISING FOR THE
DIGITAL AGE

JACOB MALHERBE

Published by Advantage, Charleston, South Carolina.
Member of Advantage Media Group.

ADVANTAGE is a registered trademark, and the Advantage colophon is a trademark of Advantage Media Group, Inc.

Printed in the United States of America.

10 9 8 7 6 5 4 3 2 1

ISBN: 978-1-59932-892-8
LCCN: 2018935308

Cover and layout design by Carly Blake.

This publication is designed to provide accurate and authoritative information in regard to the subject matter covered. It is sold with the understanding that the publisher is not engaged in rendering legal, accounting, or other professional services. If legal advice or other expert assistance is required, the services of a competent professional person should be sought.

Advantage Media Group is proud to be a part of the Tree Neutral® program. Tree Neutral offsets the number of trees consumed in the production and printing of this book by taking proactive steps such as planting trees in direct proportion to the number of trees used to print books. To learn more about Tree Neutral, please visit **www.treeneutral.com**.

Advantage Media Group is a publisher of business, self-improvement, and professional development books and online learning. We help entrepreneurs, business leaders, and professionals share their Stories, Passion, and Knowledge to help others Learn & Grow. Do you have a manuscript or book idea that you would like us to consider for publishing? Please visit **advantagefamily.com** or call **1.866.775.1696**.

To my dad, Bent Malherbe, who encouraged me to follow my dreams.
To my mom, Marie-Louise Malherbe, who taught me compassion.
To my wife for always being there for me, for her love, her kindness,
and her business mind. You and the kids are my world.

ABOUT THE AUTHOR

JACOB MALHERBE is the founder of X Social Media LLC, the first Facebook ad agency focusing exclusively on plaintiff law firms. Jacob Malherbe created his first Facebook ad in 2013 and is currently managing more than a hundred law firms' advertising on Facebook. During 2017, X Social Media ran more than four thousand ad campaigns and a hundred thousand different ads for its clients, reaching over $7.5 million in Facebook advertising. Jacob Malherbe is a frequent speaker at legal conferences about Facebook advertising for law firms. He is often referred to as the "Facebook Guy" in the industry.

TABLE OF CONTENTS

INTRODUCTION

I FIRST WITNESSED the devastating effects of the Deepwater Horizon oil spill on April 20, 2010, when I casually flipped on the local news. At first glance, it looked like something ripped from the canvas of a surreal painting—as if a fireball, spewing tornadoes of smoke, was rolling across the surface of the Gulf of Mexico.

This was long before I decided to devote my professional life to helping lawyers harness the power of Facebook advertising. There's no doubt, however, that the events that transpired in the wake of the British Petroleum (BP) oil spill had a profound effect on my life and my career, providing me with invaluable lessons as to where legal advertising was headed as well as strategies that today's lawyers must adopt in order to survive—and thrive—in a rapidly changing landscape.

That night, however, lawyers and Facebook were the furthest things from my mind. My family and I were comfortably ensconced in our new home in Navarre Beach, Florida, roughly 150 miles east of the explosion.

It was heartbreaking to watch the events unfold on live TV, especially as news trickled in regarding the lives lost on the rig. But at that moment my family and I felt completely safe. It seemed to be someone else's problem, not ours.

How wrong I turned out to be.

We'd moved to Navarre, near Pensacola, Florida, in search of solitude and a greater sense of community. To us, an island that was so remote and awe inspiring that locals called it "Florida's best-kept secret" seemed like a good place to start.

We'd vacationed there a year earlier as more than two thousand people do every summer. We were immediately enchanted by the place. Although born in Denmark, where I studied at the Copenhagen Business School, I spent much of my time in my younger years studying in foreign countries. I learned English at Oxford, French at the Collège International de Cannes, and finally Russian while living with a family in Odessa and taking private lessons from a professor from the University of Odessa.

I came to the United States to take over my father's fledgling woodworking company in Atlanta. I did what I'd set out to do. I turned my dad's struggling operation, which does high-end finish-sanding work, into a thriving business.

Yet I knew I was missing out on something. When we vacationed in Navarre, I immediately recognized how much I wanted to rid myself of the hustle and bustle of life in Atlanta.

"Let's enjoy life a little," I told my wife, Roseanna. "Let's make this place home." Our kids agreed. So we did just that, and became one of the two hundred permanent residents of Navarre Beach.

For most of my neighbors, the period from Memorial Day to Labor Day is their primary—and often *only*—opportunity to make money. During those hundred days of summer, people try to squirrel away enough funds for the whole year. They rent houses, run restaurants, sell trinkets, and generally cater to the whims of tourists.

Naively, I assumed the summer of 2010 would be no different.

But had I been able to peer beneath the surface of the waters surrounding the Deepwater Horizon spill, I might have known better. I might have been able to see, some five thousand feet down, the damaged wellhead on the rig. I might have witnessed the first traces of an estimated 3.19 million barrels of oil that spewed into the Gulf of Mexico over the course of eighty-seven days, making it the largest man-made oil spill ever recorded.[1]

It didn't take long for crystal blue waters, farther and farther away from the explosion, to begin to turn black as tar. Every day, the black mass, which seemed to glide shoreward like the shadow of some otherworldly sea beast, would drift farther east from New Orleans toward us in Navarre—toward our beaches, the economic lifeblood of our community.

To my surprise, the legal community didn't mobilize in the wake of the spill, nor did anyone take particular interest in our plight. In essence, BP was given the authority to try to fix the problem on their own. The company flew large airplanes dumping Corexit—an oil-dispersing chemical agent banned in the United Kingdom due to its danger to sea life—over the spill.[2]

Where, I wondered, were all the lawyers?

If I've discovered one glaring truth in the years since the spill, it's that most law firms are ill-equipped to leverage the power of online advertising and social media to reach those who need their services most.

In most firms, advertising dollars are squandered on antiquated technologies that are unable to reach the right clients at the right times

---

1   "Gulf Oil Spill," Ocean Portal website, Smithsonian National Museum of Natural History, retrieved Feb. 9, 2018, http://ocean.si.edu/gulf-oil-spill.

2   Marian Wang, "In Gulf Spill, BP Using Dispersants Banned in UK," ProPublica, (May 2010): https://www.propublica.org/article/In-Gulf-Spill-BP-Using-Dispersants-Banned-in-UK.

with speed or precision. Not only is the ROI on print, billboard, and TV advertising dreadfully low, it's also painfully slow—the equivalent of setting bait and trying to fish in a lake that's already been cleared.

But educating lawyers on advertising wasn't my goal back in the summer of 2010. Feeling somewhat helpless as the oil slick slinked our way, I wanted to create a website where people like my neighbors, who were confused and scared as to how the spill was going to affect their lives, could go for more information.

The truth is, I was angry. Most media stories, in my opinion, focused entirely on the long-term ecological effects of the spill while completely ignoring the immediate real-world impact on the people in its wake. And to my mind, it didn't appear that BP, which was responsible for the underwater pipeline, was showing enough concern, either. Thus, in June 2010, I decided to launch a simple blog under the domain name Bp-claim.com.

At the time, I had a moderate level of understanding of websites and experience with search engine optimization (SEO), which in layman's terms is nothing more than a series of techniques that help websites achieve high rankings on search engines. When anyone typed in the phrase "BP Claims," I wanted my blog to show up on the first page of Google.

In addition to running a website for my woodworking business, I'd created a site in the wake of 9/11 that documented the recovery of valuable coins buried beneath the rubble of the Twin Towers. It was my way of dealing with the trauma. If I could find some way to preserve what would have been a forgotten element of the 9/11 story, I'd be playing an extremely minor but personally fulfilling role in the healing process.

But unlike my 9/11 website, which was a kind of living catalog of the coins recovered from the wreckage, my BP claims blog had been built for a specific audience with specific needs in a timely manner. No matter where the victims of the spill lived, what industry they worked in, and how they were affected, I wanted to reach them—and reach them quickly.

I wanted to create a big-tent website, one that spoke directly to everyone affected by the spill. And it worked.

Because there was so much fear and uncertainty in the air, people started scouring Google for information and found my site. Readership of my blog grew that summer, especially as increasing numbers of oily clumps of residue washed up on shores along the Gulf. In Navarre, we were far from immune—the black clumps started arriving on our beaches in July.

Shortly thereafter, the "men in green" came. Recruited from across the country, workers clad in green suits with bright yellow safety vests had been hired by BP to try to scrub the beaches of the oily, black lesions that were spreading like cancer across our shores.

Traffic to my blog skyrocketed to seven hundred thousand readers by the time summer transitioned into fall.

For the first time, I realized the emotional appeal and aggregating power that strategic online communications can have. If you're a plaintiff's lawyer, imagine having all the data that I had stored on my site. Names, emails, and sometimes phone numbers of hundreds of thousands of potential plaintiffs affected by the spill, all wrapped up in a digital bow.

Today, I teach law firms across the country how to generate those content banks of potential clients using Facebook, a far less expensive and less time-consuming platform than creating and maintaining a high-end website. But, back in the summer of 2010, I was a Facebook novice. My goal, naïve as it may sound, was to make sure that everyone affected by the spill received appropriate compensation for their losses and that victims realized there was someone out there—even if it was little old me—committed to keeping them informed and advocating for their rights,

I'd been devastated to hear from some of my readers that they were jumping at minuscule $5,000 payouts. But I couldn't blame them. Many were desperate for income, no matter how meager, to make ends meet and put a Christmas present or two under the tree. Quick cash in exchange for signing away their rights to future claims would at least bide them through the holidays.

I began reaching out to lawyers, first locally and then across the country, who had successfully represented victims in tragedies like this. I'd been contacted by a few low-rent lawyers looking for a fast buck, but I declined their advances. By this time, I'd earned the trust of my readers. They were hurting, and I wanted to find someone who believed more in their plight and their cause than greedy opportunists looking for a fast payday.

Eventually, I found a lawyer named Brent Coon, of Brent Coon & Associates, in Beaumont, Texas. When I flew down to talk to Mr. Coon in December of 2010, I liked him immediately. I could tell that he had grown up in a blue collar, working-class family. He was incredibly down-to-earth, and he understood the struggles of the people I was advocating for on my website, some of whom I had come to know personally.

Even if Mr. Coon was not your traditional-looking lawyer in a fancy suit, he was the perfect lawyer to help my clients, friends, and fellow victims.

We sat down for a beer and crayfish lunch, and he told me how he'd already taken BP to court over the Texas City explosion in 2005, and how he'd pushed them to do the right thing back then. Now, he was just looking to try cases he believed in.

When I returned home, I wrote a blog post and told my readers that Mr. Coon might be a lawyer worth contacting if they were seeking a fair settlement. I uploaded his contact information, phone number, and email, and then published a blog post about him.

By the end of the BP oil spill, Mr. Coon was able to help over three thousand victims of the oil spill, coming to him directly from my website. They accounted for over 25 percent of his total caseload.

Today, with what I know about Facebook, I could have gotten him a hundred thousand clients in a fraction of the time. Using an individual website is like shining a flashlight in the dark. Leveraging Facebook is like cranking up a giant spotlight atop a lighthouse. The light not only carries far and wide, but can pierce through the darkness of cyberspace with astounding clarity and precision.

Here's why: When you use Facebook, you draw in clients. When you use a website, people have to find you—either someone tells them about the website, or they find you by accident on Google. Most arrive via search engines, which means you need to invest a lot of time and resources on SEO. But the dirty little secret about Google is that no one knows precisely what algorithms its systems use to rank sites on their search engine. It's a guessing game, and Google has the right to change their algorithm at will.

I experienced the disruptive effects of just such a change in the summer of 2013. By that time, I'd been hired by another law firm in Houston. Once word had gotten out about what I'd done for Brent Coon, others came calling. One firm in particular, D Miller and Associates, PLLC, I was interested in joining because they, too, were committed to helping claimants who'd endured the effects of the BP oil spill.

The other reason was more personal. I was—and continue to be—drawn to the challenge of solving problems, especially when they can benefit everyday men and women. I felt, through my website and my work with lawyers, that I was helping my neighbors in easily quantifiable ways.

I began to feel that I'd vacationed in Navarre, and later moved there, for a reason. I felt, in some sense, a calling. But I also realized that there were a plethora of other legal problems that I could help solve as well. I could help scores of other claimants connect with good, honest lawyers. I soon realized that I shouldn't devote my time exclusively to the BP case at the expense of others.

After all, there were plenty of other organizations, government bodies, and corporations that seemed committed to putting profits above people. Through my consultation work in Houston, I could help right other wrongs and work in different areas of the law.

My work generated instant results for the firm. I was treated like an expert and delivered in tow. When Google's algorithm suddenly changed in 2013, however, I found myself at an impasse.

To continue, I'd have to start over and try to decipher Google's new search engine parameters, which would take time and additional resources. I also knew there was nothing preventing this algorithm shakeup from happening again, either two weeks or two years down the road.

I knew the firm needed something more permanent—something that delivered results fast. Back then, Google rankings often weren't updated for three months at a time, meaning if you fell off the first page, you needed to wait three months to get back on top. Now it can be as long as eighteen months.

I've never believed in wasting that kind of time, so I began to investigate Facebook and was amazed at the speed and utility it could provide. Not only could I create individual Facebook pages for specific claimants, I could link them to websites. For my BP claims work, for example, I could send all of the people reading my blog to Facebook, creating a mass migration. And I could direct traffic in the other direction as well, creating a reverse commute from Facebook to my blog.

I realized I could do the same for a law firm—that I could generate traffic between their existing website and their Facebook pages, strengthening both. More importantly, Facebook allowed me to create advertisements that reached users who were likely to click on our ads.

In working on BP claims, I could target Facebook users in specific locations that were affected by the spill, like businesses along the coast and commercial fishermen. I could also create an audience by simply telling Facebook to look for certain keywords—like "BP oil spill," "Deepwater Horizon," and so on—and show ads to people who had an interest in the topic or who had searched for similar keywords on Google.

I could also target particular groups of users for other mass tort cases—civil action lawsuits involving one or a few defendants in a state or federal court where most plaintiffs have similar injuries from the use of the defendant's products—whether they were women who suffered complications from transvaginal mesh products, or men experiencing the adverse effects of certain blood thinners.

I was building a digital bridge between specific groups of potential clients and the firm itself. Take the vaginal mesh cases, for example. I could show advertisements that informed Facebook users that there was a product liability lawsuit against manufacturers of the mesh. If they clicked on a "Learn More" button, they would be directed to the firm's website, where they could fill out an online form.

It was a transformational moment, especially when I put my plan into action and started leveraging Facebook. The lawyers at the firm were shocked at the results. Thousands of leads came flooding in, most at $10 to $11 per lead, which cost nickels on the dollar compared to the expensive and ineffectual ad buys made for TV, radio, and print.

The firm's return on their investment in me exceeded their wildest expectations, to the point where they had to exponentially increase the number of people handling the intake of my leads from two people to twenty.

It quickly became apparent to me that these techniques shouldn't be monopolized by any one firm or relegated to any one practice area. After all, when it comes to the legal industry, lawyers always follow clients. In the early twentieth century, law firms stayed local, but as corporations went national and families became more mobile, the best local law firms transformed into national law firms. And as the world became more globalized, national law firms became global law firms.

What too many law firms currently fail to realize is that they have to take that same "follow the client" philosophy and apply it to social media and the digital realm. For years, forward-looking firms have struggled to find clients in the murky expanses of cyberspace.

Not anymore.

Facebook advertising provides them cost-effective tools to target, locate, and talk to clients with precision at a startlingly low cost.

After I left the firm in Houston and went off on my own, I found that barriers needed to be broken down. Lawyers who'd been conditioned to see Facebook as a social platform for friends and family had difficulty seeing its professional applications. The hardest part of my job was helping them unlearn what they thought they knew about Facebook, advertising, and the digital space.

I'd get bombarded with questions that I thought were common knowledge: How do I use Facebook? How do I advertise? What type of ads work? Whom do I target? How do I retarget? How do I translate digital leads into client agreements?

When their questions were properly fleshed out and they were shown, step by step, how Facebook actually works and how to leverage its advertising platform, lawyers were amazed at its power and became loyal clients.

Today, my core client list includes more than a hundred plaintiff law firms, both big and small, all over this great country. But I know there is still much work to do—and countless other law firms, including those focusing on different practices, that can benefit from these strategies.

This book has been designed to be a step-by-step guide on how to launch Facebook pages, create ads, target them to reach the right people, and then convert their responses into client contracts.

Packed within these pages are all the strategies and techniques I've gleaned from three years working in the trenches and managing over $15 million worth of Facebook ad spend. After reading it, you will know all my secrets. Hopefully, these tips will help improve the lives of claimants who need your help while improving your firm's bottom line.

If you need more hands-on training for your social media employees in the future, we offer the X Social Media Academy, an online, classroom setting course, where we go through all the processes of this book and more. You can find out how to join and learn more at http://www.xsocialacademy.com.

CHAPTER 1

The Facebook Revolution: Befriending Big Brother

IN THE WORLD OF legal advertising, time is the enemy. A minute wasted is a potential client lost. Every precious ad dollar allocated to the wrong platform that reaches the wrong audience guarantees only one thing: that a rival firm will gain a client that should have been yours.

The truth of the matter is that speed does matter. In the amount of time it takes a firm to create and mount a billboard or produce and secure a time slot for expensive TV ads, potential viewers will have swiped their way through their Facebook feeds thousands of times.

And yet there are other equally important variables to consider. Are you advertising on the right platforms? Are your ads reaching the right audience? Are you spending the right amount of money per lead—and per case? And, most importantly, are your ads directly translating into new clients?

If the golden rule of the legal industry has always been to follow your clients wherever they might go, then the guiding maxim of the advertising world has been equally straightforward: go where the eyeballs are.

In today's world, your clients—and most of the world's eyeballs, for that matter—aren't spending the majority of their time reading magazines, glancing at billboards, or even watching TV.

What they're doing, en masse, is staring at the portable, customizable TVs that they carry around in their pockets and their purses—their smartphones.

And where are they spending the majority of their time on their smartphones? One place: Facebook.

Today, there are more than two hundred million active Facebook users in the United States, with an estimated increase of 23 percent per year across the globe going forward. These aren't casual users. They're engaged followers. Recent analysis shows that one out of every five minutes spent on a mobile device is spent on Facebook.[3]

What many lawyers—and members of the general public, for that matter—don't realize is that Facebook's survival is predicated almost entirely on advertising. Currently, 98 percent of Facebook's revenues stem from advertising, a stunning percentage made possible by Facebook's unique ability to deliver targeted ads to users who will be most interested in advertisers' products or services.[4]

Therefore, if you're under the impression that Facebook is a social media platform, a means for keeping in touch with family members and old law school friends, you're only fractionally correct.

---

3   "Number of Facebook Users by Age in the US as of January 2017," Statista, (January 2017): https://www.statista.com/statistics/398136/us-facebook-user-age-groups/.

4   Rakesh Sharma, "How Does Facebook Make Money?" Investopedia, (December 2017): https://www.investopedia.com/ask/answers/120114/how-does-facebook-fb-make-money.asp.

If anything, Facebook, at its core, is a delivery system for disseminating real-time advertisements to the right people. And if you're a lawyer, it also happens to be the single greatest marketing tool ever created.

THE SITE THAT SEES ALL

If you are a Facebook user, privacy is an illusion. Whenever any of us signs up to be a member of the Facebook community, we are in essence waving our rights to privacy. Whether we want to admit to it or not, Facebook is Big Brother. It's the panopticon—an all-seeing, all-knowing social media platform that's been artfully designed to know more about you than your own spouse.

Facebook monitors pretty much all of your web traffic. If you go to a site that houses Facebook "like" and "share" buttons, Facebook not only records that you've visited the site, it also monitors what pages you've visited within that site.

And if you stay logged into Facebook while you browse Google, things get even more Orwellian, as Facebook can trace every site you visit whether it has a Facebook Trojan horse button or not.

If you have the Facebook mobile app, ask yourself this question: Do you ever log in to Facebook or do you just stay logged in all the time? If you do stay logged in 24/7, trust me when I say that the platform sees all.

Facebook's built-in trolling apparatus is central to its existence, as each of your online moves helps the site build a profile of you. Each bit of information is dropped into what we will refer to as one of Facebook's many **data buckets**.

Facebook generates thousands of different data buckets. Do you like flipping through pictures of garden parties? *There's a garden party bucket for that.* Have you been looking to buy a new backyard grill? *Good to know—into the grill bucket you go.* Redoing your house? *You're in another bucket.*

For Facebook, knowing what buckets your behaviors and interests fall into is extraordinarily valuable information. Retailers that sell flowers, grills, or wallpaper, for example, can log in to Facebook and program its advertising platform to send you targeted ads that will perfectly align with your individual online searches and Facebook posts.

After all, who's more likely to buy a Weber grill? People who have been actively typing "backyard grills" and "barbecue steak recipes" into Google, or those who have been searching for "crockpots" and "slow-cooker tips"?

The key word here is relevance. Facebook accumulates all of this information—who you are, where you live, what you do, what sites you visit—so that it can create a customized news feed for you. By the time you open up Facebook and start scrolling down your feed, Facebook has already determined which posts you're likely to read and enjoy. To be fair, what would you rather see as an advertisement if you have no other choice? Would you rather see something that interests you, or something that has no relevance to you whatsoever?

This is precisely why Facebook users are so accepting of interest-based advertising. It feels individualized—like it has been generated just for them. This AI-generated customization keeps people coming back to the site minute after minute, hour after hour, day after day. But if you could see an x-ray of this personalized news feed that we all love so much, you might be surprised at what's happening on the back end.

Advertisers can tap into the wealth of information stored by Facebook and create customized ads that reach very specific audiences. This targeting goes way beyond macro categories. The buckets that

Facebook creates are not as broad and generalized as the labels that TV networks apply to their viewers. ESPN might know that viewers who watch *SportsCenter* like sports, but what specific sports are they tuning in for? Are they looking for football highlights or NBA highlights? Same thing with, say, HGTV. Are viewers tuning in because they want to remodel their house or sell it?

Think about your particular legal practice for a moment. What buckets might interest you? If each bucket were a little pond, which would you want to go fishing in?

If you're a mass tort lawyer working on a case against a big pharmaceutical company selling pancreatic cancer drugs, you'd want to send your ads to people who have pancreatic cancer or have discussed the drug in question. If you're a disability lawyer, you might want to go looking for people who have filed disability claims or who keep visiting Social Security websites. A real estate lawyer might look for foreclosures and short sales.

Remember: Facebook monitors everything. It knows your occupation. It knows where you live, your ethnicity, your interests and behaviors, as well as what links you click on and what pictures you enlarge in your Facebook feed. Facebook recognizes which videos you watch and how much they interest you based on how long you watch them. What stories are you commenting on? What are you saying on Facebook Messenger to friends? If you're posting a great deal about travel plans, then you might magically see an Expedia advertisement appear on your feed.

Let me give you a simple example as to how Facebook's big data capabilities can be leveraged by a lawyer in real time. Let's begin by exploring the power of Facebook's advertising potential for personal injury lawyers.

Consider, for example, the events that transpired on the morning of September 29, 2016, when a commuter train careened into a Hoboken, New Jersey, train station at the height of rush hour, killing one person and inflicting injuries on more than a hundred others.

The impact of the crash collapsed support columns, spewing debris everywhere, trapping commuters beneath the wreck, and sending others to the emergency room and critical care. Chaos ensued as survivors fled the scene and emergency personnel flooded in to help survivors.

As media reports trickled in, lawyers from a firm in Hackensack immediately contacted us and asked if it was possible to send a targeted ad to as many people who might have been on that train as possible.

It was indeed possible. Using our in-house designers, we immediately began crafting an advertisement and a new Facebook page that focused exclusively on the derailment. Because the names of passengers had yet to be released, we needed to play detective and quickly determine which Facebook users should see the ad.

We started by thinking in purely geographic terms. What was the train's route? Which stations did it stop at? What were the names of the communities surrounding each stop?

In no time, we had uploaded a targeted ad with a picture of beat-up old tracks and a speeding train. The text was simple and direct—"Train Wreck Injury Claims"—accompanied by the name and phone number of the firm sponsoring the ad.

That was the first wave. Once we built an initial audience, we focused on enlarging that audience through what you'll learn is called "lookalike targeting." "Tags" can be helpful in this point of the process, and, in case you are unfamiliar, act like guideposts. You can, for example, tag someone who is in a photo that you posted. But you can also tag someone in a comment and they'll see the post.

By tagging people, Facebook's AI-generated news feed automatically detects the tag and slips our ad into their news feed. If someone was tagged in a post about the train, there is a greater likelihood they were either on the train or somehow affected by the derailment. Thus, you can see the speed and precision of Facebook advertising. It helps locate your ideal audience and delivers the ads immediately, which in this case even led to a call from an injured rider who was being treated in the hospital at that very moment.

That's one of the great draws of Facebook advertising. You can now reach people instantaneously—anytime, anywhere. You can send ads to hospital patients as they are getting wheeled to their beds with geo-targeting. You can ping a potential client as they are walking out of a courthouse. You can contact a home buyer while they are touring a foreclosed house.

Ultimately, it was the speed with which we sent the New Jersey train ad as well as our precision in targeting the right audience that made this quick turnaround possible.

Facebook advertising is extraordinarily effective for plaintiff lawyers. Failed hip replacements? Car accidents? Hernia mesh damages? Big pharma lawsuits? There are stories and strategies for every conceivable case and area of focus, but Facebook advertising can be equally effective for lawyers working in different areas of the law.

If you're a divorce lawyer, consider advertising for people who have changed their relationship to, "It's complicated," which is Facebook parlance for, "My marriage is breaking up." Or consider focusing on "interest" targets. You can ask Facebook to create an audience of people searching for "divorce attorneys," or who're posting "I'm officially single" pronouncements.

What about criminal defense attorneys? You could think along geographic lines and create an advertising ring around jails. You could send advertisements to those who have searched for bail bondsmen or visited websites describing prison life.

Let's say you've already started a case, and you're representing Uber drivers seeking restitution from the company. We could target cities and areas where Uber usage is the densest—or Uber users and drivers themselves.

Geography. Demography. Race. Occupation. Interest. Behavior. Income. Facebook has created all these macro buckets as well as thousands of subcategories.

Until now, this extraordinarily detailed information and granular data about potential clients has been beyond the reach of lawyers. It was sealed away in file cabinets and locked behind passwords on hospital computers.

It was communicated quietly outside of earshot in restaurants, near office water coolers, and at family parties. It was personal and private—unseen and ephemeral. And now it's being stored and curated by Facebook, which has amassed extraordinarily detailed dossiers on all of its users.

Facebook isn't going to hand out that valuable information for you to look at, but it has agreed to send ads to those people's phones, tablets, and computers, which I would argue is nothing less than a revolutionary moment for the legal industry.

In fact, geographic, demographic, and interest targeting only scratches the surface of what Facebook can do. In the pages that follow, we will discuss strategies for targeting people using something we call **enhanced audiences**, which enables Facebook to find hidden similarities between users. These techniques will allow you to leverage big data to find similarities between your current clients and your future clients. Once you have mastered enhanced audiences strategies, nothing can stop you from building Facebook ad campaigns that generate an incredible return on your investment.

A FIVE-MINUTE HISTORY OF LEGAL ADVERTISING

Like it or not, lawyers are facing an adapt-or-die moment. Many of the most forward-thinking firms in the country already realize this. They've seen the results; they've realized just how cost-effective and efficient Facebook legal advertising is. And, as you might expect, they see no reason to share this newfound competitive advantage with rivals or smaller law firms.

In all honesty, Facebook advertising is a see-and-you-shall-believe phenomenon. I know there are plenty of digital snake-oil salesmen out there. You've likely been pestered by countless "digital advertising experts" already—all of whom probably claim they can deliver you clients by the bushel. Their pitch is usually the same: give them a bundle of money and they'll find a way—like the Pied Piper with his magic flute—to bring an endless sea of clients marching through the door.

Chances are you've probably also been burned more times than you've seen value, especially if you practiced in the 1990s and early 2000s when great pitches were plentiful but actual results were woefully thin.

That's not to say there aren't some amazing SEO specialists and internet marketers working across the country. There certainly are. But there are a host of underperformers who go around milking law firms dry as well.

Facebook advertising is different because it's (a) extremely cost-effective, (b) lightning fast, (c) built on a platform that can target the right audience, (d) can be tested immediately without a ton of upfront costs, and (e) actually converts leads into clients.

Consider, for a moment, a brief history of legal advertising. For much of the twentieth century, the American Bar Association maintained strict prohibitions against lawyers placing ads for their services. The three Rs ruled: reputation, referrals, and results.

It was an old-boy network, all business cards and "I got the check" lunches. Who do you know? Who are your friends? What's your social standing around town?

Then came *Bates v. State Bar of Arizona*, a critical US Supreme Court decision in 1977 that ruled that the traditional bans imposed by the American Bar Association on legal advertising were unconstitutional. In its decision, SCOTUS granted states the right to determine their own guidelines regarding legal advertising.[5]

First came a trickle of ads, then a deluge. Soon, legal advertisements started popping up all over the country, in both big cities and smaller towns—everything from tiny black-and-white print in "special advertising" sections in magazines to huge, colorful ads on giant billboards erected along highways and busy thoroughfares.

For some lawyers, getting their face and phone number on TV proved to be a true game changer for their practice. After all, by the closing decades of the twentieth century, TV had become the communication medium of choice for most Americans. If you were a personal injury lawyer or workers' comp attorney, you could blanket the airwaves with empathetic David vs. Goliath ads about how you were committed to helping the little guy go to battle against large, faceless corporations.

The problem, of course, is that producing and placing a TV ad is an expensive proposition. And in time, most commercials became

---

5   Victor Li, "Legal advertising blows past $1 billion and goes viral," ABA Journal, April 2017, http://www.abajournal.com/magazine/article/legal_advertising_viral_video; Bates v. State Bar of Arizona. Oyez. Accessed February 9, 2018. https://www.oyez.org/cases/1976/76-316.

something of a blur. They all looked the same: a talking head set against the faux backdrop of the scales of justice or a classic courthouse façade. And trying to discern which station to advertise on—at what exact time—was often pure guesswork.

Some enterprising lawyers and law firms got lucky, finding a niche and translating their ad dollars into paying clients. The ROI for most firms, however, was dismally low.

When internet usage skyrocketed during the 1990s, law firms realized there was a benefit to creating websites and leveraging SEO. If, for example, a firm could make sure that their name came up on the first page of Google when someone typed the phrase "divorce lawyer," or "immigration lawyer," people were more likely to click on the firm's site and sign on as a client.

The problem, of course, is that both TV ads and traditional Google searches lead to uneven results. The advantage of TV ads is that they allow law firms to enter people's homes during commercial breaks. They're simple, empathetic, and instructive: "We can help if you call this 1-800 number." But because the format for these ads has become so unnervingly similar, they often turn away as many viewers as converted new clients.

In conducting a Google search, the user feels more in control. It's a search-and-find mission. The major drawback? Potential clients have to show initiative. They had to know they needed a lawyer, commit to hiring one, and then begin their investigation. It takes both time and work, which reduces the number of people willing to see things to their logical conclusion.

Then, as online usage surged—and on-demand TV options as well as ad-skipping technologies further eroded the reach and influence of TV ads—it became clear to some prescient law firms that the future of legal advertising was slowly but irrevocably drifting toward cyberspace.

The problem, of course, with setting up a fancy website is that you have to wait for your clients to come to you. You're not really putting your name in front of people who are getting divorced or have suffered an injury or need an immigration lawyer. You're hoping those people come to you.

What Facebook does is combine the best of both internet advertising and TV advertising into one glorious platform. First and foremost, it eliminates the problem of trying to guess which TV channels to advertise on. With Facebook, you're guaranteed impressions. The ads will emerge in the feeds of a specific group of Facebook users that you select—all of whom will be potential clients who will likely be interested in your particular services.

Will you reach the same number of people who watch the Super Bowl? No, you won't. You're going to be targeting a smaller audience, but it will be an audience of people who will be motivated to click on your ad.

It takes no effort to find a Facebook ad; whenever people scroll down their feeds, the ads come to them. You can't TiVo them, and you can't skip over them, because they're going to emerge, almost like camouflage, in your feed.

It's active advertising, targeting audiences more precisely than TV ever could, and it's less expensive and less time-consuming than TV advertising or using SEO, as even with SEO it may take some time to get your website ranked, if you even can. And most important of all, it delivers a more predictable outcome.

The fundamental question is this: Do you think your potential clients are going to go out and actively take the time and effort to find and contact your firm out of a hundred different law firms of equal stature? Or are they going to select the firm that makes things easiest for them? The firm that literally delivers an ad onto their smartphones and into a platform that they're staring at all day?

And the best part of this paradigm shift is that lawyers can do all this themselves. Unlike with TV or billboards, you don't necessarily need a middleman or broker. Let me show you why it works and how to do it.

CHAPTER 2

Why Facebook Works: A Primer for the Legal Field

WHENEVER I'M BEING cross-examined by a skeptical lawyer about the power of Facebook advertising, I often parry with a deceptively simple question: "If the overwhelming majority of your clients are on Facebook, shouldn't your law firm be as well?"

Although the answer to that question is almost universally a "yes," most slow adopters fail to realize the extent to which rival law firms are already employing comprehensive Facebook advertising strategies. Forward-thinking lawyers are, at this very moment, slipping targeted ads into people's Facebook feeds and attracting clients into their ranks at a rapid clip.

And yet, for many firms that have yet to make the leap, caution still reigns. This trepidation usually stems from a fundamental lack of understanding of three important aspects: (1) how Facebook's advertising platform works, (2) why Facebook ads are so effective, and (3) what, generally speaking, constitutes a Facebook advertising campaign.

It stands to reason that if you don't understand how the platform operates and why it's so effective, you'll be less likely to visualize what it can do.

It's like the legal industry itself. How can you try a case if you don't have a firm grasp on the underlying laws that will ultimately determine the final verdict?

So let's start with one of the foundational concepts of this book: legal ads are more effective in "push" mediums than "pull" mediums.

What's a "push" medium? Think Facebook and television. Think about mediums that literally push advertisements onto people's screens. Once you log in to Facebook and start dragging your thumb or cursor down your feed, ads will begin emerging on your news feed.

The ads will be shuffled into the waterfall of posts generated by friends, businesses, and organizations that you've "friended" and let into your private Facebook circle.

A push medium like Facebook is far different than a pull medium like Google. You have to type a search into Google's search engine for it to be effective. Users go looking for specific information and thus need to know precisely what they're looking for to gain value.

The problem is that legal clients (especially in regards to lawsuits) sometimes don't realize they have a case until they've been told they have one. Clients need someone to connect the dots for them.

Say, for instance, that someone suffers a blood clot. They get rushed to the emergency room. After hovering between life and death for twenty-four hours, they get the correct treatment and emerge from the hospital—alive, but forever changed.

Now a question: How many people who suffer from blood clots take the time to try to decipher what caused that blood clot? How many blood clot sufferers sift through the medical literature and discover that one of the medications they were taking put them at serious risk for one?

Very few people have the time—or energy—to draw connections between causes and effects. They don't realize that two plus two equals a potential lawsuit.

In order for Google to be an effective tool for these victims, they have to do a lot of investigating, i.e., "pulling" information from websites. And then, if they're fortunate enough to draw a connection, your chances of getting a call is nothing less than a roll of the dice. Given the law firms listed on Google, all you can do is hope they click on your firm's site.

Now consider what happens with an ad on Facebook. As we've already established, Facebook monitors your every move in the digital realm. And for most people, it's the first place they go to inform others that they (or someone they love) have been in an accident or have experienced a life-changing event.

Facebook knows, for instance, if you've posted a message about being rushed to the hospital with a blood clot. It knows if you've been typing the phrase "blood clot" on your phone. And it knows if you've looked up medications online, as well as countless other critical bits of information about your behavior and condition.

If you are a mass tort lawyer working on a blood clot case, you can direct your ads to people who align with these criteria. All you have to do is go into Facebook's Ads Manager and find the keywords "blood clot," "deep vein thrombosis," or "pulmonary embolism/PE" under the interest targeting, and Facebook will handle it from there.

Facebook will scan all of its data buckets, locate the best matches based on the "profile" you've created, and will generate an audience that likely will be interested in seeing an ad about blood clots.

You can determine how much you want to spend and how long you want to run the ad—perhaps continuously or for a certain time interval. Then, faster than you can say "Mark Zuckerberg," your ads start getting shuffled into people's feeds.

That's the Facebook difference. It puts ads in front of people who will be most interested in clicking on them, with a precision that other push mediums like television can't match.

Thus, you can begin to see the vast difference between a digital push platform like Facebook and a digital pull medium like Google.

On Google, potential clients have to go looking for you. On Facebook, your ads go looking for potential clients. Which of the two, in our time-strapped age, do you think potential clients are more willing to accept?

SAFE SPACES:
THE PSYCHOLOGY OF FACEBOOK

Facebook's ability to "push" ads onto the screens of potential clients is the direct result of its unique ability to generate highly customized news feeds.

If you've ever seen the film the *Social Network*, you already know that the roots of Facebook stretch back to founder Mark Zuckerberg's college days at Harvard University, when he began experimenting with computer programs that allowed perfect strangers to share information through the ether of cyberspace.

As a sophomore, he created a program called CourseMatch that helped students decide which classes to take based on input from other students. Then came a program called Facemash, which posted pairs of photographs of people and encouraged users to vote on which of the two was more attractive.[6]

By February 2004, Zuckerberg launched what was then known as "thefacebook," a new platform named after the distilled profiles of students and staff given to Harvard freshmen.[7]

The growth of Facebook, as it would later be called, was swift. Within a month, over half of Harvard's undergraduates had set up a profile. Soon, usage of the site spread across greater Boston through the Ivy Leagues, and eventually to universities across the country.[8]

Much of the reason for Facebook's success—and its utility in the realm of legal advertising—is rooted in the site's ability to tailor the content of our news feeds so that we all see posts we are likely to be interested in.

In some sense, we are the gatekeepers of our personal Facebook sites. We can choose whom we "friend," and thus tell Facebook whose posts are allowed to show up on our feeds, and we can "unfriend" anyone we like, thus banishing them from popping up on our feed.

You can create and join an endless number of private groups, each built around any topic imaginable. If you have diabetes, there's a group for that. Interested in old stamps? You'll find plenty of fellow collectors. A fan of the New York Yankees? No problem. There are Yankee groups galore.

Think of Facebook as church for the digital age. It's designed to build communities between like-minded individuals. Relationships form and, within these relationships, people launch into new conversations every minute of the day.

---

6   Jose Antonio Vargas, "The Face of Facebook," New Yorker Magazine, Sept. 20, 2010, http://www.newyorker.com/magazine/2010/09/20/the-face-of-facebook.

7   Sarah Phillips, "A Brief History of Facebook," The Guardian, July 25, 2007, https://www.theguardian.com/technology/2007/jul/25/media.newmedia.

8   Ibid.

Facebook is a tool for self-validation and, for some people, Facebook usage borders on addiction, as it constantly validates who they are or who they want to be. They need it, use it as a crutch. They feel safer within these private groups that they have been granted membership into than in the real world.

What's unique about Facebook advertising is that it allows lawyers to slip ads into these individual conversations without being perceived as an interloper. Imagine nudging yourself into the middle of a conversation at a friend's wedding in hopes of signing up a new client. What do you think would happen? You'd get shamed out of the circle before you finished your first sip of champagne.

Slipping a targeted ad into someone's private feed, however, is perfectly acceptable. Users have become so accustomed to seeing ads embedded in their feeds that they view it as an essential part of the Facebook experience.

It's the equivalent of leaving a stack of your business cards at the company water cooler or in the dining room at Uncle Joe's family birthday party. But instead of just business cards, these ads can speak directly to the needs and desires that lead people to log in to Facebook in the first place.

After all, Facebook's platform is designed to ensure that you see ads that are pertinent to you—which is precisely why people tend to pay more attention to them than TV ads.

The more an ad feels like it's been tailored to you—i.e., delivered specifically to you at a time when you need help and are feeling especially vulnerable or enraged—the more likely you are to click on it.

It's the digital equivalent of feeling a sugar craving at the grocery store and then turning around to see a perfectly wrapped Snickers bar in the candy display at checkout. Great Facebook ads are not only customized to make you feel like someone has read your mind and knows exactly what you need, they also play on your impulses.

It's human nature to assign responsibility to other parties, especially when we're feeling vulnerable. It wasn't our bodies that failed us, it was the drug that the pharmaceutical company created or the pack of cigarettes we smoked. It wasn't our fault the marriage failed, it was our spouse's fault. And so on.

As "realpolitik" as it may sound, moods and emotional states matter in the advertising world—especially in the realm of legal advertising. When you're alone in your personal Facebook feed and feeling a particular set of emotions, a well-crafted ad can give you comfort or hope. So you click on that ad—even if it's just to see where it takes you.

I know this from personal experience. Over the years, I've run tens of thousands of individual Facebook campaigns for law firms. And I can honestly say that the law firms able to create ads that generate hope—whether it's hope to avoid deportation, hope to end a tumultuous divorce, or hope to gain monetary compensation for an injury—find the greatest traction.

In short, psychology matters. It's not only the stunning array of tools that Facebook offers that draws clients toward legal advertisements, it's the emotions they feel when cocooned in the comfort of their self-designed Facebook world.

BUILDING THE RIGHT AUDIENCE: AN INTRODUCTION TO FACEBOOK'S PIXEL

Although there's a whole separate "techie" book waiting to be written about all the secretive algorithms and technologies that allow Facebook to curate your feed, Facebook is very transparent about how its advertising platform works.

Before we get into the nitty-gritty of building effective individual action pages, ads, images, and videos, it's important to begin thinking about the audience you want to reach.

When it comes to audience building, there's no more powerful tool than something called Facebook's **pixel**. Technically speaking, a Facebook pixel is a string of JavaScript code that you embed in your website. Think of it as an advanced "cookie," those digital tracking devices that help websites recognize repeat visitors to their sites.

The difference, of course, is that a Facebook pixel does far more than a cookie. Installing a pixel is super easy. You go to Facebook's Ads Manager and from there to the "Measure & Reports" tab, click on "Pixels," and then the site walks you through the process.

Facebook pixels are invisible. You can place pixels on any individual web page you want Facebook to monitor, including a law firm's landing page that asks visitors to provide contact information. Even after you've installed them on one or multiple pages, they remain invisible. No one knows they are there but you. Think of it as the ultimate snitch. It sends messages back to Facebook whenever someone visits or performs an action on your site.[9]

If you create a Facebook ad and link it to a page on your website that's been embedded with a pixel, Facebook will closely observe what happens. It will track how many people clicked on the ads, and it can also count how many people then filled out a conversion form to sign on as a client.

This is critical data, as Facebook audiences are built in tiers. First, you target what I call a **cold audience**—i.e., people whom you surmise might have an interest in your particular suite of legal

---

9   "How does the conversion pixel track conversions?" FaceBook Advertiser Help Center, retrieved Feb. 9, 2018, https://www.facebook.com/business/help/460491677335370.

services. In later chapters, we'll detail the various strategies for helping Facebook find these individuals, but for now just think of a cold audience as your initial targets.

Take, for instance, a case I personally worked on for a Houston law firm beginning in 2013. It was a lawsuit directed against the manufacturer of Actos, a drug designed to help type 2 diabetics. As evidence began to mount that Actos might be a contributing factor in bladder cancer in some diabetics, the firm launched an advertising campaign to sign up potential victims.

We began our campaign by entering key phrases—like "bladder cancer," "Actos," and "type 2 diabetes"—into Facebook's Ads Manager engine to build an initial audience. We'd created profiles of early victims who'd come forward and generated an outline of the kind of audience we were pursuing. The keywords and search criteria we provided Facebook generated an initial list of potential clients—and off our ad went.

This initial group was our cold audience. Many of these Facebook users might not have even realized that the drug they were taking (or the drug a family member or friend was taking) had a propensity to cause cancer. But thanks to Facebook, we knew that their behavior in one form or another indicated an interest in bladder cancer or Actos.

When you send out an initial wave of Facebook ads, all you can do is wait and see who clicks on them. If you're a law firm with an established database of clients, you're ahead of the game, as you can upload names and email addresses and Facebook will create a general profile for you.

If you've been doing this as long as I have, you learn how to play "Sherlock Holmes." With even the most simple clues and keywords, I'm able to feed Facebook enough information to ensure the right people see my clients' ads.

But the real power of Facebook's pixel only becomes apparent when people start clicking ads and venture toward your site. When that happens, Facebook's pixel turns into a master informant. It monitors which users are clicking on the ads, which users are exploring the site set up by the law firm, and which users are actually signing up to become clients.

All of a sudden, portions of the cold audience turn warm. Although we no longer need to send ads to users who have already registered to become clients, we do need to follow up with those who visited the site but didn't sign on to become a client—which is my definition of a **warm audience**.

By now, the initial interests, behaviors, and profiles that we fed into Facebook have been refined even more, as we've already seen who's actually clicked on the ads.

Our next step is to tell Facebook that we want to send a second wave of advertisements to profiles just like the ones we converted. And it's off to the races once again.

That's the power of Facebook. Every phase of a campaign builds on the previous one in ways that are simply not possible on other platforms.

In the Actos case, we wound up sending out four waves of advertisements, which is often the golden number when it comes to multi-district litigation cases. We sent the third wave out when favorable verdicts from bellwether trials began to come in.

Wave three is usually sent out as time is waning and we need to convince stragglers that (a) plaintiffs are winning cases, and (b) their window of opportunity for joining the suits is closing.

By this point, the precision in your targeting strategy has become so refined that you're speaking directly to the people who most likely will join your suit. You're not employing a shotgun approach anymore—you're using a highly accurate and targeted scope.

This is often followed by wave four, the so-called "last-chance ad," when all those skeptics who have dragged their feet and avoided joining the suit are presented with indisputable evidence that settlements are coming and the final window for damages is going to be shut forever.

By the close of the Actos campaign, we'd brought on 150 clients as part of the suit. It was such a success in terms of ROI—especially given that we started with $4,000 to $5,000 in ad spend—that the firm's use of Facebook advertising grew exponentially thereafter, to the point where the firm is now using it for twenty different mass tort cases. As a result, the firm spends an average of $100,000 per month on Facebook advertising—talk about a butterfly effect.

The moral of the story is that such results would not have been possible anywhere but on Facebook. Those ads were placed in front of the right set of eyes. We were able to convert ad dollars into clients because of the way Facebook can push ads into the feeds of people who are motivated to hire a lawyer. At the end of the day, Facebook works because it makes legal advertising less expensive and delivers more predictable results.

But what we've outlined so far are broad strokes; they're the roadmap as to what happens and the underlying reasons why Facebook advertising works. In order to mount a successful Facebook campaign, it's worth sweating the details. You have to know how to target precisely the right audience. You have to design informative and persuasive ads. You have to know when to use video versus still imagery. And you have to build effective individual action pages on Facebook and engaging landing page websites to ensure that new clients will find you and fill out a lead form.

Ultimately, knowing how to do all of the above will correctly and efficiently generate the best results. What follows is my secret recipe on how to do it right.

CHAPTER 3

Facebook 101: Creating Effective Individual Action Pages

THE POWER OF FACEBOOK ADVERTISING lies, above all else, in the unprecedented degree of customization it offers its users. It's a digital canvas without borders, a platform that never sleeps—and never stops looking for ways to slip ads into every nook and cranny that the Facebook platform has to offer.

In terms of ad buys, you can spend what you want, where you want to spend it. You can program your ads to be placed along the borders of a Facebook page, camouflaged into the scroll of users' news feeds, or even make them show up before the launch of videos or text on a diverse array of popular apps.

But in order to maximize the potential of the platform, you need to build an audience of **potential new clients (PNCs)** by making your presence felt on Facebook. You need to be a part of the conversation. If you're an immigration lawyer, you need to have a page devoted exclusively to issues that affect immigrants. If you're working on a mass tort lawsuit about a cancer drug with negative side effects, you better create a page that speaks directly to the users of that medication.

PNCs who click on your Facebook ads will be sent directly to a lead form on your website. But to ensure that Facebook is directing those ads to the right users, you should create content-rich individual action pages that educate, engage, and inspire them to want to hire you as their lawyer. These pages not only provide a platform for you to weigh in on the issues that are important to potential clients, they also provide you with another channel that directs Facebook users to the lead forms on your website.

Unlike an online magazine or website, you're not starting from a blank slate. Design experience is not needed because Facebook—as even the most casual of users will know—offers a click-and-fill design template. You have your **profile image** in the upper left-hand corner of your page and the long rectangular banner running across the top of the screen, which is called your **cover photo**. And of course, you have your **news feed** running down the middle of the screen—with columns bookending your feed to the left and right if you're working on a computer and not a smartphone.

It goes without saying that no single advertising strategy will meet the individual needs of all the lawyers reading this book. There is no magic formula. There is no single Facebook design and photo strategy that will be equally appealing for every practice, but there are some golden rules that are worth following.

Some strategies are of the "click-and-go" variety. They are for lawyers who just want to start advertising—and advertising *fast*—or for lawyers who simply want to experiment with the platform. Other, more advanced approaches can help you design and launch large-scale campaigns that continually gain traction and build on your previous efforts.

No matter which path you choose, success lies in fine-tuning the right balance of logic, emotion, and artistry that will appeal to your targeted audience.

If you use Facebook for your private pleasure, all of these initial steps are probably old hat to you by now. You have likely already set up one or more Facebook pages, uploaded photos, and started posting content. And yet one of the biggest mistakes that lawyers make is falling under the misconception that the strategies they employ on their personal Facebook pages are equally effective as those they should utilize when at work.

In many cases, two wholly different approaches are required.

For those who have already passed Facebook boot camp, consider this a refresher. But for those ready to build their Facebook advertising infrastructure the correct way, right from the start, here is where to begin.

STEP 1: CREATE A BUSINESS-ONLY FACEBOOK PROFILE

Chances are you have already created a personal Facebook profile page to keep up with friends and family, but if you haven't launched a professional Facebook account for your practice, building one is an essential first step. Mixing your private and professional life comes with more than its fair share of difficulties. Consider email. You likely have one email address for friends and family and a separate one for your work. Why not do the same for Facebook?

Don't grant professional acquaintances access to your Facebook profile page unless you truly trust them. In today's remarkably divided society, do you really want to turn off people who disagree with your politics, show disdain for your favorite sports team, or loathe your movie and TV preferences? Not a chance. Create a hard-and-fast border between the two and make sure it's not porous.

STEP 2: DECIDE WHETHER TO STAY INDEPENDENT OR CONNECT TO YOUR FIRM

Although some firms may restrict their lawyers from creating independent Facebook pages that are unaffiliated with the firm's main Facebook hub, it's important to decide if you want to stay independent or leverage the social media power of your law firm.

If you set up your own independent Facebook account, you have an ability to experiment with your advertising campaign away from the prying eyes of other lawyers in your firm, but you will have to do all the work yourself.

Often the better choice is to establish your page by piggybacking it onto your firm's Facebook account. Just know that you will be providing other people access to your account. For lawyers working in large firms, this approach can be beneficial, as you may be able to leverage some of the firm's IT, design, and social media resources to aid you in your campaign.

No matter which approach you choose, you are ultimately responsible for the content of your ads and your pages. You or your firm has to submit your Facebook pages and ads to your state bar. Fortunately, you can begin advertising as soon as they are submitted. If the state bar recommends changes, just make them as they come in and resubmit your ad. By that time, you will already be on the way to scooping up more clients.

STEP 3: CONSTRUCT AN EFFECTIVE MAIN FACEBOOK PAGE

There are two different types of Facebook pages that you should create before you begin generating ads. The first is a **main law firm Facebook page**, which is the equivalent of the front page of your law firm's website, and which informs visitors what exactly you do. The second is the individual action page, which is discussed in step 4.

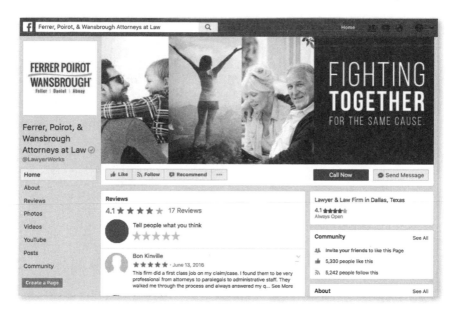

If you're part of a large law firm, your firm's main Facebook page has likely been established already and is probably being updated by the firm's IT and communications teams.

If you're running your own firm, make sure you create a main Facebook page if you don't have one already. This is the place where a firm can tout all of the professional, civic, and philanthropic work it is performing. You can profile any donations you have made in the wake of a tragedy, any honors and awards you have received, and any key and influential cases you have won.

If you're starting from scratch, remember that there are two empty spaces for images that you need to fill. The profile picture in the upper left corner of your page should be the logo of your firm or a group photograph of prominent partners. The cover photo, which stretches across the top of the screen, should be filled with an engaging, professionally shot photo that symbolizes the culture or professionalism of the firm. If your firm is focused on a single practice, upload an image that reflects your focus—i.e., images of divorce for family law, an immigration document for immigration lawyers, and so on.

Make sure to add your location, hours, contact information (phone and email), and website in the **About** section. You can add other customized information if you so desire, including a **Photos** tab if you have additional lawyers in your firm, a **Videos** tab if you are creating additional content, or a **Review** tab.

The goal of your main Facebook page is to create an aura of competence and altruism. It's about gaining trust. Use it as a rebuttal to whatever stereotypes a potential client may hold about lawyers or the legal industry in general or as evidence that you are the best lawyer for their particular legal need.

Remember that potential clients are often comparative shoppers when it comes to legal services. At some point, perhaps after they have clicked your ad, potential clients are going to do some rudimentary research. They will often look up your site on Google and type in the name of your firm on Facebook. If your main page looks and reads better than another firm's, you will often be given the benefit of the doubt.

Your main Facebook page will be one of the most accessible and convenient ways for prospective clients to research you. Hence, your page must capture your firm's intelligence and expertise. Use professional photos. Take time to copyedit your posts. And make sure to post any substantial victories that are pertinent to visitors. If you're a product liability lawyer and you just won a major round of lawsuits on a regional or national level, post it here.

If you operate a law firm focused exclusively on local clients, think along the lines of your local news broadcast. What wins have you scored within your community that you wish had been broadcast on the evening news? This is your platform to brag a bit, so make it look sleek but also sophisticated and refined.

Just remember that the absolute worst thing you can do on your main Facebook page is fail to ensure your images are the correct size. All images posted to your timeline, depending on the type of image or video you're uploading, must be a specific size and dimension to appear as normal and as desired on users' screens, both mobile and desktop views. It looks extremely unprofessional when images on a company's Facebook page are the incorrect size. Make sure to size them correctly and move on to the next step.

STEP 4: CREATE A SENSE OF COMMUNITY THROUGH INDIVIDUAL ACTION PAGES

It's equally critical to start building what we refer to as your **individual action pages.** These are pages that speak to the specific needs of the clients you are hoping to attract. Your law firm's main Facebook page is very general in nature (our law firm did X, Y, and Z), while an individual action page is very specific.

If you're a mass tort lawyer, you want to create individual action pages for each and every lawsuit you are currently pursuing, from the cancer drug that caused hair loss to the malfunctioning ignition switches that caused drivers to lose control of their cars and create accidents.

Your posts regarding the automobile accidents will have no relevance to cancer patients and vice versa. So make sure to create individual action pages for each. There's no utility, for example, in mixing a discussion involving a car ignition lawsuit with a different lawsuit focused on a cancer drug. You don't want those two topics to sit on a single page because those cases don't intertwine.

If you're an immigration lawyer, however, discussing visa applications and deportation defenses on a single individual action page may hold value, as one issue often leads to another. People want to read about the effects of losing their visa and how it can lead to deportation.

If you practice family law, create an individual page for divorce, but don't get too granular. You don't want to create individual pages for child custody, domestic abuse, child support, and divorce, because these issues often overlap and you want to focus on the correct audience, without which you'll have trouble cultivating a real community.

Remember that you're building a *community* of people with similar concerns and/or needs with these pages. You want cross dialogue, because that brings people back to that individual action page and increases your stature. If a potential client trusts you, comments on your page, and praises your work, it's more likely that someone will call you or private message you for information about the services you offer.

STEP 5: MAKE SURE YOU'RE BUILDING AN AUDIENCE

I can't stress this enough: individual action pages are crucial to a successful Facebook advertising campaign because they help you build an audience that is interested in the legal services you're offering.

By constructing individual action pages that cocoon around a particular topic—pages filled with articles, videos, and conversations around custody battles, for example—you capture the interest and imagination of potential clients. You are offering evidence that you're knowledgeable about their specific need, which increases the likelihood that they will hire you and not another, non-Facebook lawyer down the street.

Think about your audience when you create these individual action pages. If you're representing clients who suffered adverse effects from a diabetes drug, make sure to post about issues related to diabetes and the diabetes drug in question. When one diabetes sufferer finds something of note on your page, they may share the article on their feed and thus bring other diabetics to your page.

Remember the key phrase "building a community," because that's what these individual action pages do. Outside of the digital realm, lawyers tend to go to events—fundraisers, talks, community colloquiums—in order to reach a particular community. But in the realm of Facebook, what you're trying to do is post information about a particular community—diabetics, in this example—and have the diabetics come to you.

Send out an ad that directs Facebook users to these individual action pages and—voila—they will find the kind of community they have been looking for. You can run an ad campaign to get people to "like" your individual action page or engage with a post you have written. Anyone who "likes" your post can be invited to "like" or "follow" your page.

This sense of community increases the odds that they will move from your individual action page and agree to hire you as their lawyer.

STEP 6: POPULATE YOUR INDIVIDUAL ACTION PAGE WITH THE RIGHT CONTENT

If you have experience setting up a personal Facebook page and posting under your own profile, populating an individual action page should be relatively straightforward. That being said, there are some specific strategies worth employing that will help you create a community and convert as many clients as possible.

As an example, consider one of the individual action pages we established for a law firm handling a mass tort case involving Benicar, a high blood pressure medication. The lawsuit was initiated around 2011 when it was discovered that certain individuals who used Benicar began developing severe gastrointestinal problems, including, in some cases, Crohn's disease. By August 2017, the victims had won more than $300 million in settlements, but in 2011, all we had to work with was a blank Facebook template and an idea as to how to draw in potential clients. This is a simple step-by-step tutorial on what we did and why we did it.

Rule 1: Simple Titles Work

It's important to remember that Facebook is the third largest search engine on the planet, behind only Google and YouTube. For example, take an SEO (search engine optimization) approach to the title of your individual action pages.

Brevity is your friend here. Think short and to the point—five words maximum. When naming an individual action page, don't get too literary or too cute. Be direct. Think like a lawyer. In our case, we simply chose to go with the title "Benicar Lawsuit." If it had been a Xarelto lawsuit, we would have simply named it "Xarelto Lawsuit." Other keywords that work well instead of "lawsuit" are "claim," "claims," "lawyer," "attorney" (i.e., "Xarelto Claims," "Xarelto Lawyer," "Xarelto Attorney") and so on.

Rule 2: Categorize Your Page

Basically, you should treat the prompt to categorize your page as if it's asking for your profession. Type in the keyword "lawyer" or go to the drop-down box and scroll until you get to the word "legal" and click on it. This is yet another Facebook data bucket, which allows advertisers like yourself the ability to target particular professions. If you're a medical malpractice lawyer, for example, you will want to target qualifying patients with your ads. Facebook will be able to direct your ads to victims because they have willingly filled in this box. Medical malpractice lawyers target patients, not doctors, as they are the ones at fault.

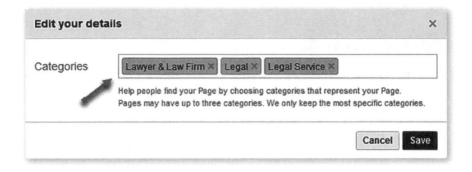

Rule 3: Upload the Right Photos

This is the point where you have to think about what types of images you want greeting visitors to your page. Think carefully about using the right photos for both your profile image and cover photo. Remember to stay within the state bar rules and to put a firm logo and principal address on all images on the page. Also remember to put a phone number (preferably a 1-800 number) on the cover photo.

Collaboration with a designer is often beneficial here, as you can get into legal trouble if you just go to Google and start plundering snapshots from random websites. Remember that you're operating within a highly visual medium. If you simply slap a makeshift photo across the top of your page, you're going to scare away potential clients. They're going to see a generic or cut-rate image at the top of the screen and immediately think, "This must be a scam."

Make sure the content of the image is relevant to the practice or  case at hand. In the case of the Benicar lawsuit, we created an illustration—in the style of the icons you see on smartphone apps—of a blood pressure cuff for our profile picture. Anyone who takes blood pressure medication has feelings about a blood pressure cuff. It's likely part of their daily routine, so it resonated with visitors.

At the same time, we chose to directly address the pain and discomfort of common side effects in our cover photo. We used a series of images—hands clutching a stomach, a woman holding her mouth like she was going to vomit, and a woman clutching her abdomen in pain.

Excessive weight loss, chronic diarrhea, vomiting, and other gastrointestinal (GI)

The goal is to make people see themselves in the images. You have to create a balanced equation. Logic plus emotion. You need a little bit of each to draw in both right-brain and left-brain thinkers.

Whatever your practice, think about symbolism and emotion. If you're a personal injury lawyer focused on car accidents, you might want to produce an image of an accident with a victim looking sad and despondent, sitting on a curb nearby. If you're a divorce lawyer, perhaps a marriage contract or family photo that's been ripped in half. Don't be afraid to pull on people's heartstrings, as long as you don't overdo it and you don't play up the emotion in both images.

Rule 4: Be Direct with Your Text

Some images speak for themselves, but in order to solidify the emotional connection you've made with your potential client, consider adding some text to flesh out the image. In the case of Benicar, it was important that we pointed out the side effects of the drug, so that people realized there might be a cause-and-effect relationship between the drug and the discomfort they were feeling. In big green letters, we simply spelled out common side effects using the phrases "excessive weight loss," "chronic diarrhea," "vomiting," and "gastrointestinal issues." This more text-heavy marketing can be accomplished in the cover photo, as we are not advertising it. On a post with an image we pay advertise, we can only use very little text in the image due to Facebook's 20 percent text rule, which you'll learn more about in chapter 6.

Use text to emphasize certain aspects of the image. Consider detailing with straightforward language. In the case of the Benicar lawsuit, studies showed how the drug elicited devastating side effects in some people. The more you can underscore that there is a movement afoot to right the wrongs caused by a particular product or incident, the more people are likely to want to be a part of that aggrieved group. It's human nature. If we've been wronged or injured, we don't want to feel like we're alone. We want to join those who have experienced similar miseries.

Think of the text as being the digital equivalent of a billboard you might see while driving down your local expressway. Think of talking points or an outline of your services. For immigration lawyers, point out that you handle visa applications. For divorce lawyers, highlight the fact that you have experience with difficult divorces. After all, few people would hire a lawyer if a separation was going smoothly, right?

STEP 7: START POSTING

You have to think ahead when it comes to Facebook advertising. There's nothing static about the medium. Unlike ads on television or those unmovable billboards over freeways, your ads will be part of an organic Facebook feed that has to be kept constantly fresh and up-to-date in real time.

When it comes to posting content, return to our analogy of an online magazine. You have to think like a journalist now. The key filter to remember, time and again, is credibility. Your first post must—without exception—come from a trusted source: perhaps a video clip from a cable network, or a news article from a respected newspaper or magazine.

Trust comes first, because when a page starts up, you have approximately zero followers. It's just a single page floating among millions of other pages. You need a bank of content that projects authority up and down your page before you go out and start welcoming people to your page via ads.

Think in layers. In the case of Benicar, if you start with a *New York Times* or *Washington Post* article outlining the medication's flaws, where do you go next? A newspaper article is informational— that's one side of the equation. Then, for the other side, how do you humanize your page? How do you project and evoke emotion?

You need to put a human face to your efforts. In the case of Benicar, are there videos that show people talking about their daily struggles? Can you drive away the fear that your page is merely a hook to lure clients and instead find a way to demonstrate that you care deeply about the topic at hand?

Vary up your posts. Clinical studies can add an aura of authority to your individual action page. Post clips of doctors talking about the dangers of the drugs and the side effects of the medication. Upload videos of clients talking about how your firm helped them.

Don't shy away from creating your own content if it's not available for reposting somewhere else. We've helped law firms create professional videos for as little as $100, including those that can run on Facebook Live. And believe me, the return on those small invest-ments can be profound in the long run.

Ask one of your lawyers to talk about the drug and its side effects on camera and upload the video to Facebook or use Facebook Live to stream it in real time, which is free and easy and can be achieved with little cost.

STEP 8: FILL IN THE FINAL DETAILS AND CREATE AN OUTSIDE WEBSITE

Once your individual action pages have been established, make sure that you create some avenue for potential clients to contact you. In some cases, it's as easy as establishing a "Call Now" button or a "Message" button. Some people prefer typing messages and others prefer using their phones, so make sure to provide people the option to do whatever is most comfortable for them.

The second option is to create a "Learn More" button. When clicked, this button will direct visitors to a sign-up form on your website—what we call a **landing page**.

In chapter 9 we will discuss the art of creating effective forms that will convert Facebook users who clicked on an ad into actual clients. Please note that it is essential—*absolutely essential*—that you create a stand-alone website outside of Facebook. The majority of lawyers already have their own websites, but you'll need to build your own landing page—for this, hire a web designer or sign up for one of the build-your-own-site services like Unbounce.com and Instapage.com.

Individual action pages and ads are built to generate interest and lead PNCs to your landing page, where they fill out lead forms and provide contact information. Firms must then convert those leads into clients, strategies for which we will discuss in chapter 9.

This is especially true for complicated lawsuits. We've worked, for example, on lawsuits involving the heating and cooling units used during open-heart surgery. The FDA has found that in some units, bacteria from the factory where they were produced laced the equipment, which sometimes produced deadly infections in people, ailments that might not have emerged as long as twelve months after surgery.

For a complicated case like this one, you want to lay out exactly what the lawsuit includes so that people can see if they qualify or not. We will discuss how to create forms that ask questions in an effective manner in chapter 5.

One last reminder: It is often necessary to place disclaimers on the bottom of your pages. These disclaimers vary widely from state to state and practice to practice, so we won't go into them here. Just remember to follow the bylines drafted by the individual state bars to stay compliant with their rules, which must be followed to ensure your ads and pages can go live and the advertising can begin.

CHAPTER 4

Foundations for Success: Digital Infrastructure and the Art of Establishing an Ad Account

NOW THAT YOU'VE CREATED your individual action pages, our goal is to ensure that your pages don't disappear into the digital ether—i.e., get lost amid the millions of other individual pages that comprise the Facebook network.

Even if you've designed the most aesthetically charming, perfectly structured, and skillfully curated individual action page ever devised, it does no good whatsoever if no one actually sees it.

The *Field of Dreams* mythos doesn't work here. Just because you've built it, doesn't mean they'll come.

To gain traction, you have to draw people to your pages to build an audience, which allows Facebook's suite of advertising tools to find PNCs and place ads on their feeds.

Although the legal field may be late to the Facebook party, other industries have been leveraging Facebook's advertising abilities for some time.

Take, for example, car dealerships. For years now, Facebook has been accumulating an extraordinary amount of personal data about its users, including information from credit-reporting agencies as to when people's car loans and leases are due to expire.

Dealerships know that when people's leases and loans come due, there is a greater chance they will look into buying new vehicles. When savvy dealers want to run a Facebook ad, they can log in to Facebook's Ads Manager hub—a central control panel for customizing your campaign—hit **Browse**, go under **Behaviors,** and look under the **Automotive** tag. There you'll find a list of behaviors related to cars and car purchases; simply click **New Vehicle Shoppers (In market)** and Facebook will optimize its ad delivery platform to find people who are considering a new car.

Detailed Targeting ❶   INCLUDE people who match at least ONE of the following ❶

| Add demographics, interests or behaviors | Suggestions | Browse |

▼ | Automotive

▶ | Motorcycle

▶ | New vehicle buyers (Near market)

▶ | New vehicle shoppers (In market)

Connections ❶   ▶ | New vehicle shoppers (Max in market)

▶ | Owners

▶ | Purchase type

▶ | Used vehicle buyers (In market)

Suddenly, car ads and sales flyers begin popping up in select news feeds, which appear to users to be perfectly timed to fit their needs. "How in the world did the local Acme Toyota dealer know I was in the market for a new car?" they wonder.

It turns out that no one was reading anyone's mind. It was all about accruing data, building an audience profile, and then allowing Facebook to use those profiles to find similar people who might show interest. That's how once devout Ford or Toyota loyalists suddenly become proud Chevy or Hyundai owners. And that's the exact same way that lawyers can quickly—and cost-effectively—generate a slew of PNCs.

If building individual action pages is the first step—the foundation of any ad push—linking those pages to Facebook's Ads Manager should be your next goal.

Think of it as the advertising equivalent of connecting your smartphone to Wi-Fi. You can have the sleekest cellphone on the market, but if it's not linked to the internet, it's not getting the power it needs to do its job. Here's a tutorial on how you can customize Facebook's Ads Manager to ensure your campaign attracts the attention of those who can most benefit from your legal services.

UNLEASH THE POWER OF THE PIXEL

The first and most important thing to do when you arrive at the Facebook Ads Manager's main page is to click on the icon for Facebook Ads—look for the icon depicting three horizontal lines—and then find the **Measure & Report** tab.

★ Frequently Used	≡ Plan	+ Create & Manage	⊿ Measure & Report	▦ Assets
Business Settings	Audience Insights	Business Manager	Ads Reporting	Audiences
Ads Manager	Campaign Planner	**Ads Manager**	Test and Learn	Images
Billing	Creative Hub	Page Posts	Analytics	Catalogs
		App Dashboard	Events Manager	Business Locations
		App Ads Helper	Pixels	
		Automated Rules	Offline Events	
			App Events	
			Custom Conversions	
			Partner Integrations	

This **Measure & Report** tab offers the ability to set up a Facebook pixel under the option that reads, fittingly enough, **Pixels**. As you may recall from chapter 1, the Facebook pixel is a string of code that acts like an advanced "cookie." It is a super spy. Once it is embedded in your individual website, it sits there quietly and begins collecting data as to who's visiting your website, what pages they are visiting, and what, if any, actions they are taking. All of this critical surveillance data is then reported back to Facebook to use as it pleases.

Ultimately, the information that this pixel collects will lower the cost of your advertising campaign, as it will help Facebook direct your ads to users who are mostly likely to require your services.

You can create one pixel per ad account, with each pixel being able to be placed on as many websites as you want to generate date. (If you want look at different kinds of data and users, you can add up to ten different pixels by upgrading to Facebook's business manager service.) To begin, just follow along with Facebook's prompts. It will ask you to name the pixel. When you are done naming it, click the "Create" button.

Facebook will then offer you three options, each accompanied by short videos that walk you through how to easily install the code.

Use an Integration or Tag Manager

These are a series of handy plug-ins for third-party website services like SquareSpace, Wix, and Woo Commerce. If your website was constructed by one of these services, this is the option to choose.

Manually Install the Code Itself

This is the DIY option. You will manually copy and paste the code into the header of your website. Instructions are provided by Facebook itself.

Email Instructions to a Developer

If you are working with a designer, this will email him or her your unique Facebook pixel code. Although instructions will be provided, designers with Facebook experience should know how to do this already.

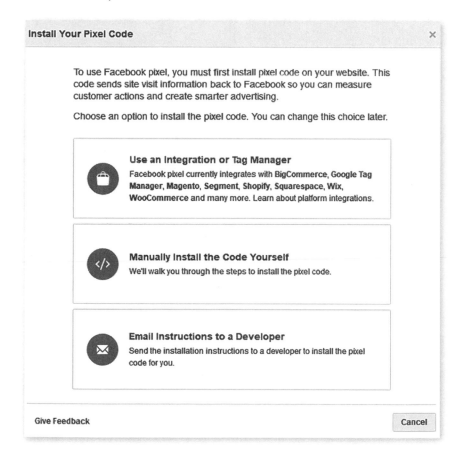

It's absolutely critical, in my opinion, for lawyers to slightly modify Facebook's pixel code so that it can be placed on the "thank you" page that pops up *after* a potential new client has filled out a lead form. Unlike, for example, an e-commerce retailer, who wants to monitor how many people are clicking on a particular product, lawyers want to know two things: (1) who is visiting their site and,

(2) more importantly, who is actually filling out a form and providing contact information. Remember: they don't agree to become a client; they agree to talk to the law firm to see if the firm can assist.

Here is a look at the modifications we have made to Facebook's code. You will see a portion of the original code first, followed by the modified code. Simply add this additional text to Facebook's original code.

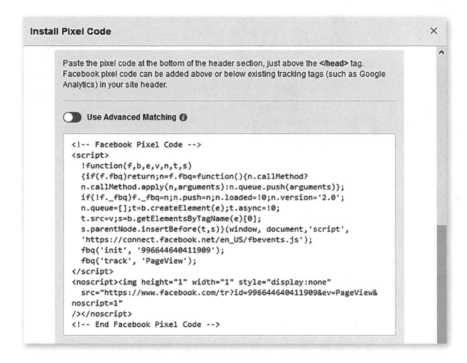

2 **Add the events you'd like to track**

Select the event categories that are meaningful to your business, and choose how you'd like to track them.

- **Purchase**
- **Generate Lead**
- **Complete Registration**
- **Add Payment Info**
- **Add to Cart**
- **Add to Wishlist**
- **Initiate Checkout**
- **Search**
- **View Content**

Don't see an event that fits? **Learn more about custom events.**

```
<!-- Facebook Pixel Code -->
<script>
!function(f,b,e,v,n,t,s){if(f.fbq)return;n=f.fbq=function(){n.callMethod?
n.callMethod.apply(n,arguments):n.queue.push(arguments)};if(!f._fbq)f._fbq=n;
n.push=n;n.loaded=!0;n.version='2.0';n.queue=[];t=b.createElement(e);t.async=!0;
t.src=v;s=b.getElementsByTagName(e)[0];s.parentNode.insertBefore(t,s)}(window,
document,'script','https://connect.facebook.net/en_US/fbevents.js');
fbq('init', '996644640411909');
fbq('track', 'PageView');
fbq('track', 'Lead');</script>
<noscript><img height="1" width="1" style="display:none"
src="https://www.facebook.com/tr?id=996644640411909&ev=PageView&noscript=1"
/></noscript>
<!-- DO NOT MODIFY -->
<!-- End Facebook Pixel Code -->
```

Once you have modified the code, a pixel will be embedded in your "thank you" page and Facebook will begin collecting information about who filled out your form. This information will be relayed back to Facebook's main database, which will be able to create a lookalike audience. It will analyze all of your conversions and look for patterns, isolating a new audience of people likely to be interested in your services as well.

Once Facebook has begun this process, you can direct your ads to this new group of people—an **enhanced audience**—thus improving your ROI and reducing your overall advertising spend. These savings and the ultra-precise targeting of lookalike audiences is only possible due to Facebook's pixel and the backend platform.

INDIVIDUAL ACTION OR COLLABORATIVE WORK?

Think of the Ads Manager hub as the digital equivalent of a sales broker who wants to sell you print, billboard, radio, or television ads. If you wanted to advertise on one of those more-antiquated mediums, you would sit down with a sales rep and discuss your advertising goals, where and when you'd like to place your ads, how much you'd like to spend, and how long you'd like to advertise.

Facebook's Ads Manager offers the exact same guidance by prompting you with preestablished questions. It's a simple step-by-step process. You answer a question and the Ads Manager sends you the next question. It's as easy as working with tax preparation software—for example, when TurboTax asks if you own a home with a mortgage or if you made charitable contributions this year.

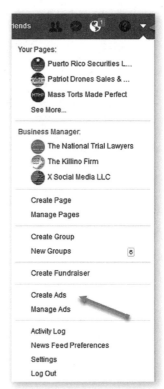

There are two different ways to access the Ads Manager program. The quick and easy approach, which allows you to get started right away but puts all the onus on you to handle your advertising campaign, is to go to your personal Facebook account and find the downward arrow in the top right side of the page. Look for **Create Ads** and get started.

This approach allows you to move quickly and run a simple campaign. If you're new to Facebook advertising or are simply experimenting, this is a good place to start. But in all honesty, it pales in comparison to the options available to you if you go to that same downward arrow and find the phrase **Advertising on Facebook**, which directs you to https://business.facebook.com, a more advanced and powerful portal that can aid you in creating collaborative campaigns.

This portal is a collaborative hub—sort of like a cloud-based Google Docs platform—where you can create a dashboard and allow professionals to handle particular aspects of your campaign.

If you're running ads linked to different individual action pages, all you have to do is add your individual action pages to this central hub—either through a drop-down box or by pasting in the URL of your page—and it gets connected to your preferences.

As the operator of your Facebook account, you have total control. You can farm out access to individual facets of your campaign to outside users. If you want to hire a full-service Facebook ad agency like ours, you can stipulate how much money you want to spend and then allow us to go get you your clients. If you want to divvy up your outsourced work, you can hire someone to create your individual action pages and ads, someone else to work on audience building, and someone else to help turn leads into clients.

In most cases, law firms are so shocked by the number of potential clients that Facebook can generate that they eventually need help just to keep up with the influx. Working on the campaign via https://business.facebook.com allows you to be the operator of the site, offering access to others to collaborate on your campaign.

NAVIGATING FACEBOOK'S ADS MANAGER

No matter what path you choose, Facebook will ask you for some form of payment to move on. Once you provide your credit card information, you unlock the door to Facebook's advertising engine. Now it's time to click the **Create an Ad** tab; you will be presented with a screen that looks like this:

What's your marketing objective? Help: Choosing an Objective		
Auction ● Reach and Frequency ●		
Awareness	**Consideration**	**Conversion**
Brand awareness	Traffic	Conversions
Reach	Engagement	Catalog sales
	App installs	Store visits
	Video views	
	Lead generation	
	Messages	

It's at this point that Facebook will prompt you with your first question: *What's Your Marketing Objective?* You'll see three columns—**Awareness**, **Consideration**, **Conversion**—each with multiple pre-generated prompts that you can choose. Here's a primer on what each button means, as well as the pros and cons of each selection.

Column A: Awareness

BRAND AWARENESS: Click this box if you're interested in trying to brand yourself as the go-to firm for a particular legal practice. If you want your firm to become known for work in a specific area of the law, whether it's custody battles or deportation defenses, this is the button to click. It's all about repetition and finding people who will be interested in your services. The more Facebook users see your law firm's name and interact with your ads, the more traction you will receive. This is the way to get your name out and become part of discussions within Facebook.

REACH: Similar to brand awareness but with one major difference, this campaign strategy is all about reaching as many people as possible, whether or not Facebook is sure they will be interested in your services. It's about casting a large net and seeing what you can pull in. If you know you're targeting a large pool of people—say a criminal defense attorney geo-targeting everybody who comes within a mile radius of a prison—what you're really looking for is reach, so click here.

Column B: Consideration

TRAFFIC: This can be a wise selection if you need to drive traffic over to your law firm's website when you have a particularly weighty legal matter that requires extra explanation. It's really designed to herd people to a site outside of Facebook. It's not about ensuring that visitors perform a particular action on your site—like fill out a form—but about getting them to your landing page. As a result, if you want clients to get to your website so that they can contact your office by phone, click here.

ENGAGEMENT: Click this objective if one of your chief objectives is to get people to "like," share, and comment on your posts. When people interact with a particular post, it becomes more visible to their friends. Engagement strategies are invaluable when you're trying to find a small number of individuals—the needles in the haystacks— who may be hiding within Facebook.

For example, if you're looking for people who have been diagnosed with a rare cancer (such as acute myeloid leukemia), it's going to be difficult to put in broad search criteria to find them. You need to let their friends do the work and push your ads in their direction through "likes," shares, and posts. In the case of myeloid leukemia, we can target people who have been exposed to risks in their workplace and then sit back and let them reach out to friends and other family members.

APP INSTALL: While not often of critical importance for lawyers, if your law firm has a mobile app and you want to encourage people to install it on their phone, this is an optimizer for that.

VIDEO VIEWS: If your ad materials are primarily composed of videos, this is designed to optimize your chance of traction. Our testing has shown, however, that the engagement tab works as effectively and at a lower price point.

Column C: Conversion

CONVERSIONS: This is the box we most often encourage law firms to click. I apply the **Conversions** feature 90 percent of the time when

I work with my law firm clients. We ask Facebook to optimize for conversions (i.e., not just the clicking of the ad, but the filling out of the lead form). These "conversions" are reported back to Facebook via its pixel—provided you have placed the modified pixel on your "thank you" page after people fill out a lead. This tells Facebook that we need more people like the person who just filled out the form, which empowers Facebook's algorithm to find similar users. If you're just starting out, begin here.

CATALOG SALES: This option is used by people who have online stores or car dealerships but is not often used by attorneys. This is normally an e-commerce objective. Skip it.

STORE VISITS: Again, this is an e-commerce objective, not for attorneys. Ignore.

As you can imagine, there is no single magic bullet formula that is applicable to every firm. Each lawyer, working in their particular practice and region, can come to their own conclusion as to what is best for them. When we sit down with our legal clients for consultation, we have a thorough conversation about each of these tabs and help determine which is the best fit for their particular needs, but in most cases clicking on **Conversions** is the way to go.

CONTINUING THE PROCESS: AD ACCOUNT AND AD SET INFORMATION

Once you have determined your marketing objective and clicked the appropriate prompt, Facebook will direct you to answer an additional set of questions under the header **Set Up Ad Account**. These questions are very self-explanatory: the country you reside in, the currency you will be using, and your time zone. It's all very intuitive and should take less than a minute to properly address.

You will then proceed to the next tab—**Ad Set**—which offers three additional prompts. Here's an exploration of each.

PAGE: If you have multiple individual action pages—perhaps a page for a cancer drug lawsuit, a different page for a lawsuit regarding high blood pressure, and so on—you simply go to the drop-down menu and click the page that applies to this current advertising campaign.

AUDIENCE: This allows you to narrow your search to reach particular audiences. We will delve more deeply into how to find and capture your ideal audience in the next chapter. Turn to page seventy-five for a thorough explanation.

PLACEMENTS: This is an important step, as Facebook's default choice is the **Automatic Placement** option. In this case, don't follow Facebook's advice. Instead, choose the **Edit Placement** option.

The **Edit Placement** option allows you to select where you want your ads to appear as opposed to letting Facebook choose. You definitely want your ads to appear on both mobile phones (80 percent of Facebook clicks) and desktops (20 percent of clicks). You want to include desktop views because many potential clients, especially older adults, continue to use their desktops when researching law firms on Facebook.

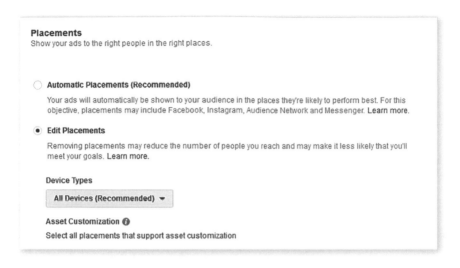

You don't want to waste your money on placing your ads in the right-hand column for the desktops, as we from experience haven't realized many conversions from right-hand side ads. People just don't seem to pay much attention to them. In addition, we've found that visitors who do click through to your landing page from these ads do so mostly out of curiosity, not because they really need your service, and therefore don't spend a lot of time on the site—and thus didn't qualify as quality PNCs. This can cause the data your pixel gathers to become diluted, encouraging Facebook to target people who aren't really interested in your services.

Whether you choose to advertise on Instagram is up to you. You have to ask yourself whether the majority of your potential audience is on Instagram to begin with. In addition, Instagram is only optimized for images, so vital text that gets people to click on an image doesn't translate. I recommend that lawyers stay away from Instagram.

In addition, if you are a beginner, you should unclick any boxes that allocate ad dollars to Facebook's Audience Network. In layman's terms, Facebook's Audience Network is a suite of affiliates that will publish your ads as displayed on their apps. Out of all the places you can advertise, this is the cheapest option, but the quality of traffic on these apps is not great.

BUDGET & SCHEDULE: One of the unique advantages of Facebook is that it allows you to set how many ad dollars you want to spend per day—look for the tab that says **Daily Budget**—or set an upper limit on the total amount of money you'd like to spend over the lifetime of your campaign with the **Lifetime Budget** option.

How much capital you choose to allocate to your ad campaign is entirely up to you. You can set an average daily budget of $50 or max out your entire campaign at $50. There is no upper threshold as to what you can spend, but the floor is $5 per day. (But if you only plan on spending $5 per day, you should seriously reconsider why you are advertising in the first place!)

What's important to remember is that your daily budget is an average spend. If Facebook's algorithm notices a lot of visitors who fit your perfect profile on Friday, it may use $6. Then on Saturday, when a greater number of people are off enjoying their weekend, it may spend only $4. Facebook will never spend more than 25 percent over your daily budget in a single day, however, which ensures it can remain within striking distance of your budget.

If you set a top line number for your lifetime budget—or if you simply want to limit the length of your daily spend—you can use the drop-down box to tell Facebook when you want your ad campaign to launch and when you want it to end. This is as easy as buying a plane ticket online, where you choose what day your initial flight leaves and what day you will be coming home on your return flight.

In choosing this lifetime budget option, Facebook merely divides your total spend by the total number of days you wish to advertise. For example, a $100 lifetime spend over ten days ensures that you will be spending roughly $10 a day over that period.

While you may be tempted to be ultra-thrifty with the amount of money that you allocate to your advertising campaign, remember that Facebook gets smarter as a campaign goes on. It may start with millions of users but then whittle that number down to the core group of Facebook users who are most likely to click on your ads, so you want to allocate enough resources to ensure Facebook can find your ideal client.

You will notice one large tab that remains in the bottom of the screen—the **Ad** tab. This will offer a final set of questions that pertain to the actual ads you want to post.

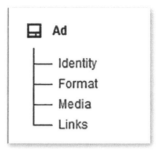

We will cover everything you need to know about ads in chapter 6, but for now we still have to address the all-important **Audience** tab—in the **Ad Set** menu—which ensures that your ads reach the right users.

As we will see in the next chapter, which explores the critical techniques of targeting, the more data that you provide Facebook in this section, the quicker it will find your ideal audience and start generating new clients. The better you become at feeding Facebook with the right data, the easier it will be for the platform to target the right users, thus lowering the amount of ad dollars you need to spend.

CHAPTER 5

Finding Your Audience: Tips for Targeting Future Clients

IF I COULD ENSURE that lawyers learned just one skill—out of all the advertising strategies outlined in this book—it would be an ability to effectively target audiences on Facebook.

I can't stress this enough: finding—and continually refining—the best possible audience is the key to finding success with Facebook advertising. The more you can zero in on specific groups of people who are interested in your services, the quicker you're going to welcome new clients and see incredible returns on your investment.

Let's return to our billboard analogy for a moment. If you were to consider purchasing a billboard ad, where would you begin?

You might begin with the old real estate maxim, "location, location, location," right? Perhaps you'd seek to erect a billboard on an expressway that regularly experiences heavy traffic. Or look for space in a public transportation hub, or near a busy intersection with lots of pedestrians, cars, and bicyclists.

At the same time, you have to consider what type of audience (age, interests, behaviors) you want to see your billboard. Who, in other words, is likely to buy the products or services you're advertising?

As a lawyer, you might shy away from targeting millennials, who tend not to use a lot of legal services. Instead you might think about people who are middle-aged or older.

You might think about demographic information, perhaps targeting people of a particular profession (perhaps truckers if there is a lawsuit involving big rigs) or have certain health concerns (diabetics, if a lawsuit stems from a particular diabetes medication).

Each practice has its own ideal audience. If you're an immigration lawyer, you might want to focus more on urban areas. If you're a part of a big tobacco lawsuit, you need to consider behaviors (and target smokers). If you're a father's rights attorney, look for interest tags or identity markers (you'd want to look for divorced fathers).

With traditional ads, you need to get a bit lucky to find those individuals. If you pour your money into a TV ad on *Judge Judy*, you're likely trying to reach people who aren't working during the day. But how do you know who's watching that show on a particular day?

If you run a radio ad, you're going to pay top dollar to run it during rush hour, when most people are in their cars. But questions still abound: which day and which station? In the past, legal advertising was a bit like throwing a huge net into the water and hoping it scooped up some worthwhile fish.

Facebook advertising is different, as you can direct your ads to a more targeted and interested audience. With Facebook, you don't have to worry about rush hour or prime time slots, because people are going to check their feed throughout the day. And you don't have to worry about spending an inordinate amount of money researching your audience, because Facebook's ad tools are constantly performing their own research, distilling down Facebook's vast user base into a highly concentrated group of interested parties who need your legal services. In order to find that ideal audience, here's what you have to do.

THE PERFECT MATCH: CREATING AN AUDIENCE PROFILE

By this point, you should have already checked a number of things off your to-do list. You've set up individual action pages, opened a Facebook advertising account, and begun answering prompts in Facebook's Ads Manager. We discussed establishing objectives as well as determining proper ad placements, budgets, and schedules in the previous chapter. This leaves only one all-important tab under the **Ad Set** menu: the **Audience** tab.

To begin, consider how you'd describe your ideal client. Create a rough sketch in your mind regarding the age, location, socioeconomic status, interests, and behaviors of the people you want to reach.

If you possess a list of current clients, upload their email addresses or phone numbers into the "audience" section on Facebook—more on this later. Select the option to advertise to a defined demographic—see page eighty—and the platform will find the individual Facebook profiles of each person. From this raw audience of current clients, you can now ask Facebook to begin looking for a list of users with similar backgrounds, what we refer to as a **lookalike audience**. But for now, let's just assume you're starting from scratch. Begin by clicking the **Create an Audience** tab. The macro search fields that Facebook provides include the following:

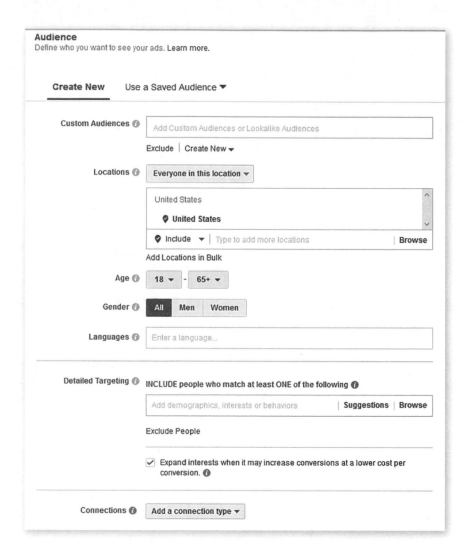

Age

Think of this as a sliding scale. You can advertise to a defined demographic: whatever age group you like, from eighteen-year-olds all the way up to seniors aged sixty-five and over.

The more you can narrow down your audience search, the better. Take, for instance, a personal injury lawyer. Although young people may get into more accidents, you want to represent people who were injured but not at fault, which means you should avoid targeting young drivers (who are often at fault in an accident) and focus instead on drivers over thirty years old. Whatever your practice, your primary clients usually fall into a specific age group. Enter that range here.

Location

This is pure geo-targeting. Do you want to allow Facebook to go looking for clients across the globe, just in the United States, or only in a particular city or state? If you're seeking clients who took a particular medication, you'll probably want to search across the whole country. Local lawyers may wish to limit searches to a smaller and more distinctly defined area.

Let's stay with the personal injury example for a moment and focus on personal injury suits, where your practice demographics could include clients involved in car accidents. Almost anyone can be in a car accident, so where do you begin? You could launch a campaign that reaches everybody who owns a car within ten or twenty miles of your office location. But an even more effective strategy might involve geo-targeting area hospitals and telling Facebook to send your ads to anyone within a one-mile radius of a hospital.

What you're doing is drawing a ring around medical facilities where people will go after suffering an injury. Think about all the time spent waiting for doctors in an emergency room or waiting room. A personal injury campaign could also be done with anyone who owns a car within a ten- to twenty-mile perimeter of your office location.

What do injured parties—as well as their family members—do during that time? They pull out their cell phones. If you can send those victims and their family members an ad, your chances of welcoming a new client to your practice go up exponentially.

Gender

Do you want to target both men and women or only a single sex? Facebook's internal statistics show that Facebook usage is pretty much split down the middle. Although these percentages tend to vacillate a bit, roughly 52 percent of Facebook activity is performed by women and 48 percent by men.

In the case of medical issues, our own research has indicated that women tend to closely monitor their own health more than men as well as oversee the health needs of their husbands. It is women, we've found, who often fill out client forms for their husbands when it comes to medical lawsuits. Out of the two hundred thousand health-related leads we have helped law firms acquire through Facebook advertising, somewhere near 70 percent have been women.

Languages

Generally, it's best to leave this section blank—although there may be instances when it's worth your time and ad dollars to pursue clients of a particular ethnic group. Most law firms target English-speaking audiences, but a Spanish-language ad directed at Spanish-speaking individuals can produce positive results. When it comes to large lawsuits, consider different ethnic communities that might have been affected. The BP oil spill affected numerous Vietnamese fishermen, so we found success employing Vietnamese-language ads.

DETAILED TARGETING: DEMOGRAPHICS, BEHAVIORS, AND INTERESTS

The next section—**Detailed Targeting**—is especially beneficial to lawyers hoping to build a strong initial audience, as it provides Facebook with keywords to search its database. The options here are almost limitless.

Detailed Targeting ⓘ — INCLUDE people who match at least ONE of the following ⓘ

| Add demographics, interests or behaviors | Suggestions | Browse |

Exclude People

☑ Expand interests when it may increase conversions at a lower cost per conversion. ⓘ

Let me give you an example: When I was asked to help a law firm find potential clients injured as the result of driving cars with faulty General Motors (GM) ignition switches (as well as individuals who owned Volkswagen [VW] diesel cars with improper emissions systems), we targeted beyond macro search categories like age, gender, and geographic location. We had to make Facebook search for people who owned these particular makes. We found plaintiffs by typing in the models of GM or VW vehicles into the **Behaviors** box (see below), and Facebook began locating which of its users owned those cars.

The big takeaway? The more you can pinpoint your ideal audience, the more Facebook will ensure that the right users will see your ads. Here are some examples of how to leverage these tools.

Detailed Targeting ⓘ — INCLUDE people who match at least ONE of the following ⓘ

| Add demographics, interests or behaviors | Suggestions | Browse |

▶ Demographics ⓘ
▶ Interests ⓘ
▶ Behaviors ⓘ
▶ More Categories ⓘ

Connections ⓘ — Add a connection type ▾

Save This Audience

Demographics

Facebook allows you to search for the kind of deeply granular demographic information that would make the US Census Bureau blush. You can narrow your audience search by applying search tags for everything from particular educational levels or an individual profession to political affiliation or the state of someone's relationship.

EXAMPLES OF DEMOGRAPHIC TARGETING: Lawyers looking for NCAA concussions cases can target athletes who played concussion-inducing sports. Individuals in certain professions who just changed jobs are often targeted in whistleblowing cases, while those seeking hurricane claims can focus on Facebook users who are homeowners in particular parts of the country. Also consider demographic targeting when working on corporate cases, like the 2015 Halliburton overtime settlement. In our search to find people who could join the settlement, we went in and directly targeted Halliburton employees. Soon, viable potential new clients came pouring in.

Interests

Retail advertisers focus a great deal on interest tags, as they want to sell football gear to football fans and specialty hamburgers to people who love fast food. But lawyers should not overlook this section, as it allows Facebook to focus on particular keywords that might emerge in a post.

EXAMPLES OF INTEREST TARGETING: Personal injury lawyers might want to search for keywords that are connected with accidents (whiplash, traffic accident, rear-end collision, head-on collision), while mass tort firms could focus on words like "hospital," "cancer," "diabetics," "hip," and "knee." Remember that you can link together words with conjunctions like "or" and "and." Applying the tags "hip" and "hospital" will get you better results than either of these alone. The downside? Facebook is receiving more and more heat for cataloging and providing this information to advertisers, so don't be surprised if some keywords in the interest targeting field disappear over time.

Behaviors

In our previous mention of GM and VW lawsuits, we were discussing behavior-based targeting. This is another particularly useful category, which allows lawyers to search for everything from a particular type of food or drink potential clients enjoy to their preferred hobbies and pastimes. The more you can imagine what actions your ideal audience might perform, the more you will be able to pinpoint your search.

EXAMPLES OF BEHAVIOR TARGETS: If you're an immigration lawyer, think about the advantages of clicking the **Expats** tag. If you're in the personal injury field, you can search for people who love motorcycles (perhaps even "motorcycles" and "hospital"). But don't be afraid to get creative. People tend to give money to medical charities because either (a) they had a health scare, or (b) someone in their family did. Thus, if you're looking for cancer patients, look into charity tags.

When we oversaw a Monsanto GMO lawsuit, we looked for people who had an interest in farming. When we were launching a talcum powder lawsuit, the **Multicultural Affinity** target proved useful. Data showed that the use of talcum powder within the African-American community was higher than in other demographics, so we focused many of our ads on African-American Facebook users.

Please note that you can also exclude certain people—click the **Exclude People** tag—from receiving your ads. Thus you can increase your chances of finding the right people by not wasting money showing your ads to those who wouldn't have any interest in the first place.

You will also note two other options that add more specificity to your targeting. You can click a box that reads **Expand Interests When It May Increase Post Engagement at a Lower Cost.** This will allow Facebook to begin refining your audience based on Facebook's own data and algorithms.

In addition, you will also see a **Connections** tag. You have three types of connections you can highlight:

FACEBOOK PAGES: You can request that Facebook target people who have "liked" your Facebook page or target the friends of people who have "liked" your Facebook page. Or you can request that it avoid targeting people who have "liked" your page altogether.

APPS: This option usually isn't pertinent to law firms. It would prime Facebook to target particular users or friends of users who use your app.

EVENTS: This might be pertinent to lawyers who stage a particular event, including town hall meetings. If someone agrees to go to a talk you gave about a particular lawsuit, it may be helpful to target these people, as having an ad show up in their feed after the event may be a friendly reminder that they should visit your site.

When you have filled out all the appropriate forms, click the **Save This Audience** button to inform Facebook of your audience preferences.

A SHORTCUT TO SUCCESS: CREATING A CUSTOM AUDIENCE

When it comes to building a Facebook audience, there's only one golden rule: the more detailed information you can feed Facebook, the more quickly and efficiently the platform will find you future clients.

One of the easiest ways for a firm to begin generating a customized audience is to use the information they already possess: the names, emails, and phone numbers of people the firm has already represented. In the Facebook world, this is "red meat" data. There's no better way to build a strong audience profile than by leaning on a list of people who have already chosen your law firm to represent them.

In order to upload your client list to Facebook, click the **Create a New Audience** tab and look for the **Custom Audience** option.

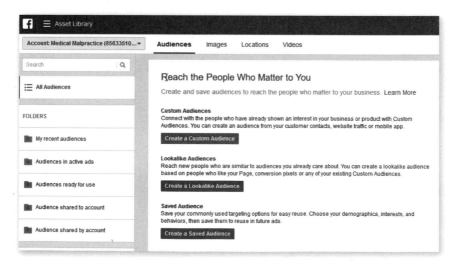

The easiest way to upload the information is to select the **Customer File**, which has an icon of a Rolodex card next to it.

How do you want to create this audience?

Reach people who have a relationship with your business, whether they are existing customers or people who have interacted with your business on Facebook or other platforms.

Customer File
Use a customer file to match your customers with people on Facebook and create an audience from the matches. The data will be hashed prior to upload.

Website Traffic
Create a list of people who visited your website or took specific actions using Facebook Pixel.

App Activity
Create a list of people who launched your app or game, or took specific actions.

Offline Activity [NEW]
Create a list of people who interacted with your business in-store, by phone, or through other offline channels.

Engagement [UPDATED]
Create a list of people who engaged with your content on Facebook or Instagram.

This process is secure and the details about your customers will be kept private.

Cancel

You will now see another set of options.

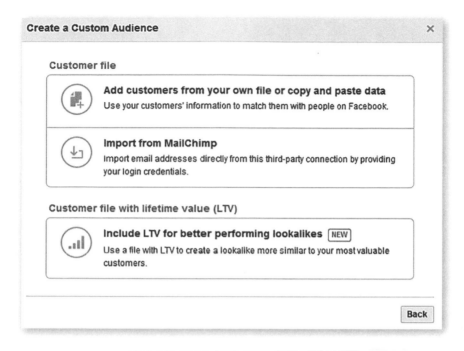

ADD CUSTOMERS FROM YOUR OWN FILE OR COPY AND PASTE DATA: This is the easy way to upload a list. It's self-explanatory. You can either copy and paste client information or simply upload a spreadsheet.

IMPORT FROM MAILCHIMP: This is an option for users who utilize a digital newsletter program, MailChimp, that is not often used by law firms.

INCLUDE LTV FOR BETTER PERFORMING LOOKALIKES: This is a worthy option, as it allows Facebook to begin looking for users who have similar profiles as the audience you have uploaded.

Once you select the **Add Customers from Your Own File or Copy and Paste Data**, you will be ushered through a series of easy-to-follow steps to help you transfer your client list.

Step 1: Add Customer List

Facebook makes it easy for you to upload whatever data you may have on your current clients. Copy and paste as much information as you can. Options include first and last name; address with zip code; email; phone number; date of birth; gender; age. But it's best to stick to names, emails, and phone numbers, as people's addresses are always changing and sometimes aren't updated on personal profiles.

If you have stored this information on a spreadsheet (either TXT or CSV file), it's even easier to create a custom audience. All you have to do is upload the files and Facebook will convert them for you. The next series of steps merely acts as a safety net in ensuring that the platform has properly processed your information.

Step 2: Edit Data Mapping

Don't be intimidated by the techie term "data mapping." All Facebook is trying to do here is make sure that it has dropped the right information into the right data buckets. It wants you to verify that no one's first name has slipped into its bucket of last names and that no rogue addresses have been misinterpreted as phone numbers. If you've used a spreadsheet, all of your client information should fall into the right categories. And if you just stick to phone numbers, names, and email addresses, Facebook processes this information correctly.

Step 3: Hashed Upload and Creation

A hashed upload means that Facebook actively scours its pages to look for the people you uploaded. But it also shields you from seeing whom exactly they found.

Step 4: Next Steps

Now you want to ensure that Facebook starts looking for potential clients who are similar to your current clients, so click on the **Create a Lookalike Audience** tab.

Create a Lookalike Audience ⊠

Find new people on Facebook who are similar to your existing audiences. **Learn more.**

Source ❶ | Choose a Custom Audience or a Page.

Create new ▾

Location ❶ | Search for countries or regions to target | **Browse**

Audience Size ❶

0 1 2 3 4 5 6 7 8 9 10 % of countries

Audience size ranges from 1% to 10% of the total population in the countries you choose, with 1% being those who most closely match your source.

Show Advanced Options ▾

Cancel | Create Audience

Facebook generates a lookalike audience by delving into all the data that Facebook has gathered about the people you just uploaded into the system. It's looking for patterns. Do the majority of your clients live in a certain place, fall into a certain age group, or share common interests, behaviors, or particular demographic information?

Facebook's willingness to sift through all of its data to find people that match up with your current clients is one the marvels of the platform. It does all the hard work. It finds similarities and turns around and says, "You should advertise to these people because they are very similar to your own clients."

After all, it's in Facebook's interest to help advertisers match up their ads with interested parties. The more that people become conditioned to seeing ads show up in their feeds, the more they will accept it as part and parcel of being on Facebook. This allows Facebook to continue to populate its ads within feeds, driving up profits.

It's a rather brilliant strategy, because it's a win-win for everyone involved. Users are shown ads that align with their needs and interests, while advertisers love that they can generate interest and traction at such a low cost. And Facebook watches its ad revenues skyrocket.

A SECOND LOOK: AN EARLY LOOK AT LOOKALIKE TARGETING

As we will see in chapter 7, you can create lookalike audiences based on different categories and by gathering information about who you've converted into clients from your initial audience.

It should be noted that you can create a lookalike audience just for the people who "liked" a post on your individual action page. You can make a lookalike audience for people who watched 25 percent, 50 percent, or 75 percent of a video you posted. And thanks to Facebook's ingenious pixel embedded in your website, you can make lookalike audiences for anyone who visits your site or fills out a form.

If you haven't installed your Facebook pixel—see page fifty-seven—now is the time to do so. I say this because if you've already placed your pixel on your website, you can begin to create a customized audience solely from the people who found your website.

Think for a moment about the power of that pixel. Before you've even launched your individual action page and tried to draw people to it and convert them into clients, Facebook has been watching who has made their way to your website purely through Google searches.

A majority of these "visitors" who have actively searched and reached your site online are likely interested enough in legal services that they performed a search and clicked on your site. Facebook knows who these people are and will allow you to create a custom audience out of these people.

You can then take this core group of interested visitors and place an ad in their feeds. All of a sudden, these curious internet surfers see the name of your law firm in their feed and your mere presence on Facebook acts as incentive to consider your services again.

It's an excellent way to begin targeting a core group of likely clients as you work on creating effective ads, the focus of our next chapter.

CHAPTER 6

Building a Better Billboard: Creating Effective Facebook Ads

SUCCESSFUL FACEBOOK ADS are neither nuanced nor subtle. Quite the contrary. Instead, a good Facebook ad is one that stops people dead in their tracks as they scroll through their news feeds. Think about how quickly people flick their thumbs up and down their smartphones or how they glide their cursors up and down their feeds while surfing the internet on their desktops. A good ad impedes that super-fast Facebook finger motion. It distracts. It teases. It compels you to slow down and read.

You have ad agencies across the country gouging people based on the misconception that Facebook ads should be complex and nuanced, the digital equivalent of the high-end ads you see on television or those oh-so-perfect print ads you see in glossy magazines.

Avoid all that noise and nonsense. If anything, effective Facebook ads for legal services should be clean and simple. They should evoke emotions as well as tap into a Facebook user's desire to know more, stay in the loop, or attain financial justice. As a lawyer, you know what has motivated people to hire you in the past. Leveraging that experience in creating an ad is half the battle.

Before you begin thinking about design elements like color, text, image selection, and the like, think about the psychology of your ideal audience. Do you want to encourage action? Do you want to educate? Do you want to evoke empathy?

Ads are a means to an end, not the end themselves. They are placed in people's feeds to lead them to your website landing page, where they can learn more about your services or fill out a lead firm. Remember that the goal is to generate conversions. So make sure you maintain continuity, in terms of look and feel, between your ad, individual action pages, and landing page. What compels someone to click on your ad should be mirrored and reinforced on your individual action page, which is another channel directing people to your landing page.

Furthermore, remember that individual action pages should engender a sense of community. They should be safe spaces where visitors feel they are among like-minded souls who share their values, needs, and concerns. Make sure people see you as a conduit for easing their pain or righting a wrong. If you do, they will click on to your site, where leads turn into paying clients.

NEW AND OLD: EXISTING POSTS VS. FRESH ADS

If you've been following the process outlined in this book, you've worked your way through most of the tabs and the majority of the fields on Facebook's Ads Manager page. We've discussed campaign objectives as well as most of the offerings on the **Ad Set** tab, from creating an initial audience and deciding on placement options to determining a budget and schedule. This leaves a single tab: the **Ad** tab.

Once you click on the **Ad** tab, you will once again be guided to a series of open fields, starting with the first and easiest option: the **Ad Name** prompt. Go ahead and choose whatever easy-to-remember moniker you'd like and then move on to the more impactful next step: the decision over whether to **Create a New Ad** or **Use an Existing Post**.

Ad Name ❶	IVC Filter Ad 1	Advanced Options
Create Ad	Use Existing Post	

In many ways, this choice is pretty self-explanatory—you can create an entirely new ad from scratch or you can choose to repurpose an existing post that you've already created and transform it into a Facebook ad.

There are, as you might expect, pros and cons to each of these approaches. I suggest beginners repurpose an existing post and allow Facebook to turn it into an advertisement. After all, you've already begun posting content to your individual action pages, so why not save time and resources and use what you already have?

The main benefit of repurposing is familiarity. If the post has gained traction on your individual action page, it's bound to garner interest when it's slipped into the individual feeds of PNCs.

The cons of repurposing? If the post isn't a sleek one, no one is going to click it in the first place. In addition, people who have a negative reaction to your post can eviscerate your work with negative comments—think phrases like "ambulance chaser," "greedy lawyers at work," and the like—before you can delete them, which is why you should make it a priority to regularly monitor your page and delete and ban negative comments and their posters.

If you choose to create a new ad, you can pay more attention to the niceties of what you are creating. It's customized content for a customized need, which is designed to lead people, step by step, to your website.

Think about how ads work on TV. You might see a riveting Apple commercial on TV, which impels you to go to Apple's website. While there, you might see or hear echoes of the ad (perhaps a single frame from the ad or a similar color scheme or song), but you won't see the exact same ad.

When you create a custom ad, you can build on the momentum you've generated in users' feeds and then lean on different content in your action page to seal the deal and get them over to that all-important new client form on your website.

The cons of new ads? When you create one, that particular advertisement will not show up on your individual action page, thus people will not have the chance to directly comment on that ad. Often users will see it once, click on it, and never see it again.

Just remember that whether you choose to create your own ad or use an existing post, many of the same rules apply in terms of the variables and templates that Facebook offers you.

If you create your own ad, Facebook will ask—under the **Format** field—whether you want to create an ad that is a single image, a single video, a carousel of images (images that automatically cycle one after the other), a slideshow (one image strung after another like an old-fashioned slide projector), or a collection (a grid of small images grouped together).

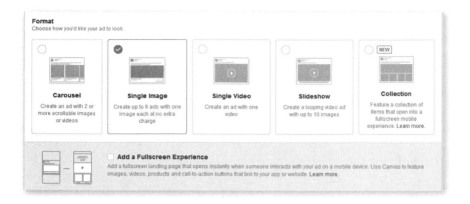

Although slideshows can be used, lawyers really want to decide between two options: either the **Single Image** or the **Single Video**. Ultimately, the simplicity and familiarity of these two options tend to yield the best results.

FINDING THE RIGHT LOOK: HOW TO BUILD A SUCCESSFUL AD USING STATIC IMAGES

As noted earlier, most images on the web are not free. Even if you've stumbled across an online image that you feel would be perfect for an ad, avoid the temptation to copy and paste it into Facebook. You don't own it, and therefore you can't use it.

Instead of poaching images, I encourage all DIY Facebook advertisers to subscribe to a stock image service, especially sites like Shutterstock, ThinkStock, and Istock, as you need to possess commercial rights to any image to publish it.

Once again, individual state bar rules vary, but often you will need to tell your in-firm designer to put your law firm's logo and principal address in the image before publishing it.

If you hire a firm like ours to do all that work, we possess—and can develop—our own customized images. We also have in-house designers who handle all the restrictions imposed by individual state bars.

If you're on your own, your best approach is to pay a monthly fee to gain access to a strong database of images and start sifting through them.

No matter what particular image you choose, it's important to remember some of Facebook's ad guidelines.

Restriction 1

Your image must be 1,200 × 628 pixels in size with an image ratio of 1.91:1—no exceptions allowed. Any other size will make your post look unprofessional, as the image will not fill up the full width of the image box in your Facebook post.

Above: incorrectly-sized image
Right: correctly-sized image

Restriction 2

Your image cannot be deemed shock-worthy or insensitive, nor can it portray handicapped individuals in a negative way. While Facebook is constantly adjusting and readjusting its advertising restrictions, there are some images that will simply never see the light of day. Grisly photos of surgery or car accidents, or snapshots taken during a tragedy (such as people ducking during the 2017 Las Vegas mass shooting) won't be accepted as ads. Neither, it should be noted, are images of people deemed to have a "perfect body image" (i.e., flat stomach, big muscles, a perfect figure, etc.) or photos of handicapped people who are in peril (such as a person in a wheelchair who is stranded on the side of a road).

Restriction 3

No more than 20 percent of your ad can be text unless you want to be hit with an extra surcharge. In the past, Facebook didn't allow anyone to post an image that was heavy on text. Now, it discourages the practice by tacking on additional fees for anyone who goes text crazy. The best practice remains the same: let your image tell the story and put up a "Learn More" button on the image to direct people to your landing page.

Restriction 4

Text must be written in the third person. Although your typical law firm ad often begins with the line "If you or a loved one experienced..." this is prohibited on Facebook. Instead, you will have to dress up your writing to say something like, "People who took X drug and experienced Y side effects can now file a claim." The whole idea is to ensure that people reading the text don't feel like the ad is being directed at them personally.

Remember that text should be added both above and below the image. Treat the text above the image as if it were a post. I encourage clients to use emojis and large capital red Xs or exclamation points to catch people's attention. And make sure to comfort them with the text you type ("Victims may be eligible for financial compensation for their losses") or give them direction ("Click 'Learn More' to file a claim now").

It should be noted that most people pay very close attention to the text underneath the image, as it is in a larger font than what comes below and is meant to act as a "title" to the image. You want this to be short and snappy. Think about titles like "Unfair Overtime Lawsuit," "Interior Vena Cava Filter Lawsuit," and "DACA Cases Welcome." Then fill in the subhead ("People implanted with an IVC filter between 2007 and 2015, click to learn more and file a claim.")

Think of short but powerful phrases that will resonate with your clients, such as "Don't Suffer in Silence," or "Don't Be Silent," or "Protect Your Rights." In the end, it's a balanced equation: short and sweet beneath the photo, more encouraging and longer explanations above.

THE PERFECT SHOT: IMAGE SELECTION CASE STUDIES

When you begin combing through image banks and subscription service archives, it's important to remember a few rules of thumb. Here are three golden strategies that have produced positive results for our legal clients across the country.

Strategy 1: Let the Image Tell Part of the Story.

You don't want to graft too much text onto the image. You want it to be iconic but also mysterious and engaging. The only text that we often emboss onto the images themselves are the words "Learn More." What you're trying to do is pique someone's curiosity and encourage them to click on the image out of interest or empathy, so let the image do its job.

CASE STUDY: Consider the work we did on behalf of a number of law firms working on lawsuits involving Zofran, a morning-sickness medication for pregnant women. Although the medication has been in use for some time, it was discovered that the medication could be absorbed into the placenta and cause heart defects in babies developing in their mothers' wombs.

As you can imagine, this is a very delicate and emotional issue. You have to be very careful when it comes to image selection in any lawsuit involving young children. What we did find was a deeply emotional image of a crying mother holding her child in her arms. The child looked beautiful and healthy. So viewers couldn't help but wonder why she was crying.

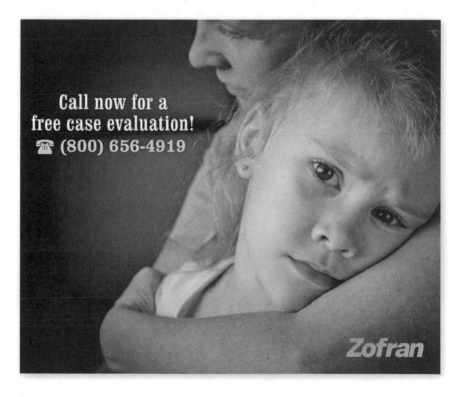

It was emotional and mysterious enough that a lot of Zofran users clicked the image. And when they got to our website landing page, a number of those viewers filled out a form, giving our law firm client valuable leads. Other viewers commented and forwarded the posts on to other people. Soon it went viral. The amazing thing? Some four hundred and thirty thousand people saw an ad that we only directly showed to a little more than two hundred thousand people. When it comes to advertising, there's nothing better than free traffic.

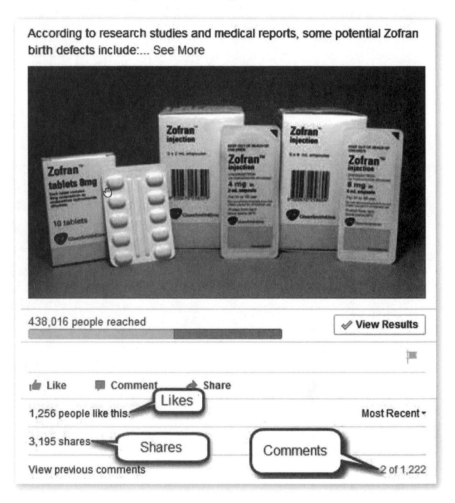

Strategy 2: Use Bright Colors.

If the goal of a Facebook ad is to literally pull people's eyes to your ad as they are scrolling through their feed, focus your attention on rich, striking colors. Avoid any ad with pale blues, grays, or sandy colors that can blend in with Facebook's own color scheme. You want pops of red, orange, aquas, and deep greens. Pick an image or illustration that literally pops off the screen and screams for attention.

CASE STUDY: We worked with several law firms seeking hernia mesh clients. Hundreds of thousands of people every year suffer from hernias, which are often treated by inserting a thin mesh screen that prevents the injury from poking through their skin. When the material within these meshes breaks down, complications can arise, including the need for additional surgical procedures.

When running ads for law firms, we used illustrations of the hernia itself, using striking yellow and orange hues to capture the seriousness of the injury. Facebook users stopped cold when they saw that image, likely because it was so different from the sunny, happy photos in the rest of their feed. We built an air of mystery. "What exactly is that image?" some people wondered. But others saw themselves in the image—either the pain they were feeling or what they feared they might experience in the future—and clicked over to our site to fill out new client forms. In the span of just nine months, we culled over forty thousand hernia mesh leads at the very low price of $20 to $30 per lead.

Strategy 3: Make It Timely.

At the risk of giving away a company secret, remember that an image can simply be a set of words positioned against a colorful backdrop. You've likely seen these types of posts crop up recently all over Facebook. They are attention getters: short and sweet. One of the most effective two-word phrases that a lawyer can ever use is "Breaking News," as people have been conditioned by TV to immediately stop what they are doing and pay attention. Naturally, you'll want to bookend this "Breaking News" graphic with text above and below, describing what that breaking news might be—remembering that Facebook has 20 percent text rule with such images. Perhaps it's a successful verdict, a new FDA warning, or a major courtroom victory. Remember to give Facebook users just enough information to whet their desire to read more, so don't supply the whole story. Just tease a little and let them come to you.

CASE STUDY: Some time ago, manufacturers started to develop retrievable IVC filters, a filter implanted in a patient's body after they experienced a pulmonary embolism. Temporary IVC filters were designed to be quickly implanted, then retrieved within six months or replaced when they began to degrade. These filters were never built to stay in for the long term. As a result, some of these filters stopped catching clots, some would adhere to veins, and some would break down, sending metal shards into patients' lungs or hearts, killing them. For some people, these IVC filters initially saved their lives but later became a ticking time bomb that could explode at any time.

Whenever a new study was completed, showing the rate and frequency with which these would break down, we'd use a "Breaking News" lure and call people's attention to the findings. If someone had—or knew someone who had—an IVC filter, they immediately clicked on that ad. People described it as a four-step process of enlightenment. The first stage was, "What's going on here?" The second was shock as they read the short description, the third was the decision to click on the ad and begin reading more on the individual action page, and the fourth was to click on the website and sign up as clients.

As a result, we were able to take in more than fifteen thousand leads, which is a substantial number when you consider the relatively small number of people who have IVC filters. The amazing thing, from my clients' perspective, was the low cost—on average, it cost our clients a mere $100 to $150 a lead.

ROLL TAPE: VIDEO-BASED AD STRATEGIES

Facebook has a vested interest in encouraging video-based advertisements. The more the platform can encourage people to watch videos, the longer people will stay on the site and the more Facebook can charge for advertising. After all, you can glance at an image, but if you create videos that take a while to watch, you're exponentially boosting visit times.

For lawyers, auto-play video ads can be attractive because they incentivize people to stop scrolling through their feeds. You see a bunch of static photos in your feed, but sharp video tends to attract more eyeballs.

The downside, of course, is that producing a video ad is a great deal more expensive than producing a static ad. In fact, we've been contacted by firms that shelled out so much money on what they perceived to be a "perfect" ad that they didn't have enough advertising capital to properly run the ad in the long run.

My advice is to employ video ads when an issue is so complicated that it's imperative that you explain to potential clients what is actually going on. Think for example of the website Investopedia, which launched short videos that deciphered complex concepts like mortgage-backed securities and derivatives.

I recommend taking the same approach when you need to educate people on how they might qualify for a complex lawsuit. Videos work really well in helping people understand how new medical findings may affect their lives or their health.

Let's return, for example, to the Zofran case that we discussed earlier. Our images were successful, but we also created video-based ads that spoke to millions of moms who took Zofran. They described what the medication could do inside a woman's body, and we also used existing footage of a news reporter interviewing a mom who described how shocked she was to discover that her baby had a heart defect.

More than anything else, the video was meant to inform Facebook users about the hidden connections between Zofran and heart defects. We realized that a small majority of those who took the drug knew that this was a possibility. Our goal was to help build a bridge of understanding for these mothers—to help them connect dot A with dot B. "Wait a minute," some users said to themselves. "My baby has a heart defect, and I was on Zofran. Maybe I should be part of this lawsuit."

After watching an effective video and feeling a personal connection to these findings, people can't help but click on the "Learn More" button to see where it might lead.

 Zofran Lawsuit Settlement   •••
Published by Jacob Malherbe [?] · February 23, 2016 · ◉

Over 200 lawsuits allege that pregnant mothers prescribed Zofran, or a generic equivalent, caused them to have babies born with congenital birth defects.

Jon and Clara Rickman, of the Birmingham area, are plaintiffs in one such lawsuit. They say their baby, Nicholas, was born with congenital heart defects after his mother took the generic form of Zofran, called "ondansetron," to alleviate her morning sickness during her first trimester.

Our Zofran Attorneys are available for ... See More

Zofran: Looking beyond the label
Over 200 lawsuits allege that pregnant mothers prescribed Zofran, or a generic equivalent, caused them to have babies born with congenital birth defects. In this special report, Lydia Hu takes a lo...
WBRC.COM

I therefore encourage lawyers to consider videos when they (a) need to educate, (b) need to help people determine if they qualify for a complicated lawsuit, or (c) are working on extremely lucrative lawsuits.

Take the famous mesothelioma cases you see advertised on billboards and television all the time. Years ago, some producers of products made from asbestos cut a deal to avoid bankruptcy by placing a percentage of their assets into a mesothelioma fund that paid out victims. If you work on mesothelioma cases, you know that, depending on a claimant's age, people can get anywhere from $2 million to $10 million with a court victory.

For lawyers working on mesothelioma cases, it's worth launching video ads because they hit all three targets. These lawyers need to educate users about the hidden connections between mesothelioma and certain workplaces (like Navy shipyards or job sites where brake pads are handled); they need to ensure that respondents qualify for the lawsuit; and the payouts are huge. That's why we oversaw the creation of video content that broke down how asbestos caused mesothelioma and built individual action pages filled with statistics, data, stories, interviews, and TV reports.

Since there are only three thousand confirmed mesothelioma cases a year, attorneys are willing to pay between $50,000 and $100,000 for one client. And it's Facebook that allows them to find those clients as efficiently as possible.

COMPLETING THE AD

Whether you choose to convert an existing post into an ad or create a new one from scratch, you still need to fill in all the remaining fields in the **Ad** tab menu. These are very self-explanatory tasks. Under the **Identity** tree, ensure that you have linked your ad to the correct individual action page, and if you want to link to an Instagram account, that option is offered as well.

What's important is that you click on the blue text that says **Show Advanced Options** at the bottom of your screen. Once again, it doesn't matter if you've chosen to create an ad from a post or create an ad from scratch. You want to click that option, as it will allow you to "Track All Your Conversions from my Facebook Pixel" (i.e., all the people who went from your ad to your website and filled out a lead form).

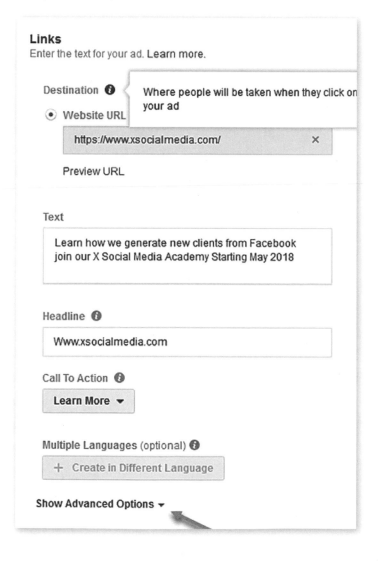

Hide Advanced Options ▲

Display Link (optional) ℹ

> Enter the link as you want people to see it in your ad

News Feed Link Description ℹ

View Tags (optional) ℹ

URL Parameters (optional) ℹ

> Ex: key1=value1&key2=value2

Conversion Tracking

Select one or more options for conversion tracking. You'll see
the results in Ads Manager along with ad performance data.

🎚 Facebook Pixel ℹ ⬅

> ● **X Social Media LLC's Pixel**
> ID:1221309364581830

App Events ℹ   Set Up

Offline Events ℹ   Set Up

This is a critical step, as you want your Facebook Pixel to be
able to report the kinds of Facebook users who are filling out lead
forms so that you can then pinpoint a lookalike audience. All you
have to do is copy and paste the address of your website into the
box and you're done. Double-check what your ad looks like in the
preview box to your right, publish it, and then turn your attention to
lookalike targeting, which is the focus of our next chapter.

CHAPTER 7

Broaden Your Audience with Lookalike Targeting

THROUGHOUT THE YEARS, I've helped countless law firms run Facebook ad campaigns for everything from mass tort medical lawsuits to individual personal injury victims. Through it all, one glaring misconception emerges more often than any other.

"If another lawyer in my field is already advertising on Facebook," the skeptics tell me, "then there's no way I will be able to find additional clients."

Part of this fear is rooted in a basic misunderstanding of how deeply Facebook has ingrained itself into our daily lives. Remember the sheer number of people who are on the platform. Facebook boasts more than two billion users worldwide—and more than 214 million monthly users in the United States alone.

That's such a staggering figure that many people fail to realize just how many different interest circles, niches, and discussion groups are operating within Facebook at this very moment.

If you take the size of Facebook's audience and compare it to the rather small number of people who are effectively advertising to these users—especially the minuscule number of lawyers doing so—you understand the true untapped potential here.

I note this because even lawyers who have been conducting Facebook campaigns for some time often overlook the power of a smart **lookalike targeting** strategy.

In layman's terms, lookalike targeting is a way to take the initial audience that you built in chapter 5 and use it as a springboard to find lookalike audiences that will be interested in your ads. The better you become at lookalike targeting, the less money you will spend as a campaign continues and the more your targeted users will be converted into clients.

Lookalike targeting is about retrieving user data and then turning around and using that data to find the right people. It's a chain reaction. The more you advertise on Facebook, the more data you collect. Increased data helps you build a more ideal audience. And the more you can advertise to that ideal audience, the more clients you're going to bring into the fold.

This much is undeniable: *Your clients are on Facebook.* And they are looking—most likely on a daily basis—at their news feeds, where you are placing your ads. In this regard, it's extraordinarily different than TV, radio, or billboards, where advertising guarantees a lawyer virtually nothing. Think for a moment about the hundreds of TV channels, all the different radio stations on the dial, and the almost limitless number of places you can place a billboard.

Your clients don't own these spaces or channels. They are owned by outside parties. But your future clients certainly "own and operate" their own Facebook feeds. And as a result, they pay a lot of attention to the words and images that appear on those feeds.

Here's an indisputable fact: If you were to open up your computer, place this book beside you, and begin launching a Facebook campaign today, you'd still be getting in on the ground floor. You'd still be ahead of the game in relation to 95 percent of your peers in the legal industry.

Despite its stratospheric growth, Facebook remains a young technology and an emerging media titan. It's still evolving. Don't assume that months from now Facebook won't be gaining ground in the streaming video race, creating its own content, purchasing movies and TV shows, and offering all sorts of other media that will keep people fixated on their feeds.

In short, if you learn how to utilize Facebook's advertising system now, you're learning how to advertise on one of the most—if not *the* most—dynamic ad platforms of the future. Facebook is moving into the television and media space with sports, shows, and movies. Consider, for a moment, the appeal of TV advertising on Facebook given all the information the platform has on its users.

It's going to be a game changer, especially for law firms, and don't be surprised if Facebook does to TV what TV did to radio or newspapers. That's why if you perfect your Facebook lookalike targeting skills now, you'll be able to reap the benefits of these strategies for the entirety of your career.

DATA CENTRAL: THE AUDIENCE INSIGHTS TOOL

In essence, Facebook's **Audience Insights** tool is the number-crunching big data epicenter of the platform. All of the data that Facebook mines from its site and all those pixels that individual users have embedded in their websites goes to this central repository and is divvied up into different data buckets.

Facebook divides its own audience up into three segments: (1) everyone on Facebook, (2) people connected to your page, and (3) custom audiences that you created.

You can choose which groups you want to study. The macro bucket of all Facebook users is a bit large for lawyers to effectively mine. And studying just those people who are connected to your page is a little narrow. But peering into what Facebook has gleaned about the *custom audiences* that you've created is one of the most effective shortcuts for finding PNCs that is available to lawyers today.

When you click on the "Audience Insights" button, you'll see five main tabs, each offering different subsets of data.

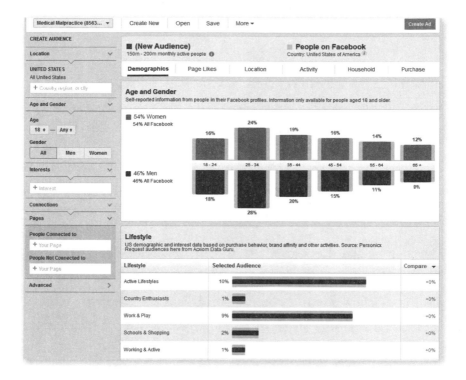

DEMOGRAPHICS gives you information on a given audience's *Age and Gender, Lifestyle* (i.e., interests and behaviors), *Relationship Status, Education Level,* and *Job Title.*

PAGE LIKES shows you what individual Facebook pages your audience is visiting in terms of categories (do they look up charities, restaurants, or department stores?) as well as the individual pages they have "liked" (Goodwill, Pizza Hut, Macy's).

LOCATION breaks down information regarding the cities and countries where your audience lives as well as the languages they use on the platform.

ACTIVITY helps you understand the actions that your audience takes on Facebook. Are they, for instance, clicking ads, "liking" pages or posts, or sharing posts? In addition, this tab details what kind of devices (smartphones, tables, desktops) a given audience is using to access the platform.

HOUSEHOLD provides information about your audience's household, with regards to overall size and income, in addition to data about the value of people's homes and what types of credit cards they use.

PURCHASE outlines your audience's spending habits, whether they are shopping online or in brick-and-mortar stores as well as what they tend to spend money on, including whether they are in the market for a car.

You can take the customized audience that you've created and use Facebook's Audience Insights tool to drill down and discover patterns, which will allow you to target a different audience during your next round of ads. Does, for instance, 80 percent of your audience shop at Walmart? Does 90 percent show an interest in diabetes? Is the majority of your audience male or female? Are most thirty to forty years old or sixty-five to seventy-five?

The great thing about this tool is that it shines the light on hidden commonalities you wouldn't know otherwise. It's a kind of open-source pattern recognition device—one being offered completely free of charge.

This data is extremely valuable for a law firm even beyond the ad campaign itself. If you're a local divorce lawyer, for instance, and the Audience Insights tool tells you that 70 percent of your clients are between thirty and forty years old, you know you've found a niche. There is something about the way you present yourself and your services that is appealing to that demographic, so you should speak at events and gatherings filled with people in that age range, send out targeted email blasts, or form marketing plans with this group in mind.

On the other hand, you may want to change your marketing or ad approach to broaden your audience. The options are virtually limitless, but in the end, the direct result is more clients and lower advertising prices.

Take, for example, an advertising campaign we spearheaded for a lawsuit related to a diabetes drug, Invokana. In June 2017, the FDA released information warning that people who took the drug might be at higher risk for amputations. For mass tort lawyers, this was a golden opportunity, as the potential returns were huge.

Our client was willing to spend as much as $5,000 per client, because payouts from the lawsuit for each individual could potentially be $200,000 or more per patient. After all, if the drug did cause damage, we were talking about people who had to have their limbs amputated and could be stuck in a wheelchair for the rest of their life. How can you put a price tag on that?

Unfortunately, actually finding Invokana users who had suffered from these side effects was no easy task—that is, until they turned to us and our Facebook strategy.

Obviously, we could build an initial audience out of behavioral and interest tags related to diabetes and Invokana. But once we initiated the campaign, we began turning our attention to Facebook's Audience Insights tool.

We found that a series of retailers' names began popping up time and again within this initial audience. As it turned out, these amputees had to shop at specialty stores that sold clothing for people who had lost a leg, foot, or other limb. In addition, this group also displayed a great deal of activity around certain companies that sold ramps and other wheelchair accessories.

We now had a new set of interests and behaviors we could target during our second round of advertising. So we targeted our advertising efforts around the names of the retail stores that kept emerging in the feeds of our initial audience.

In the end, we were able to find scores of amputees who had been on Invokana, few of which would have been found had it not been for Facebook's Audience Insights tool.

Even though finding Invokana clients via advertising was a fool's errand in some people's eyes, we delivered results, bringing in over fifty clients, each with claims that could bring in $200,000 or more per individual. Do the math on that and you understand the value of Facebook lookalike targeting.

LOOK A SECOND TIME: LOOKALIKE TARGETING STRATEGIES

If lookalike targeting is the art of taking an audience that you already have established and finding a group of similar Facebook users, then there's no need to limit your targeting strategies just to the Audience Insights tool.

Each Facebook ad and pixel that you've set up is more than just a vehicle to get people to your new client submission form; it's also a data trap. Facebook is monitoring who interacts with your posts, who clicks your ads, and who has gone all the way and filled out a form on your site.

Don't just glance at that information; use it. Never assume you've done your job once you've uploaded your client list or created an initial audience.

Instead, keep using the data that Facebook is offering you to refine your audience or create new lookalike audiences. That's how you take the millions of Facebook users on the platform and begin dividing them up, audience by audience, into smaller groups of people who need your legal services.

To begin lookalike targeting, return to the Ads Manager and look for the **Audience** tab under the **Ad Set** menu. Click **Custom Audiences**.

You will now see a familiar screen, the exact same screen you might have clicked through when you uploaded your client Rolodex to the platform. Only this time, instead of clicking **Customer File**, you can click one of the other options below.

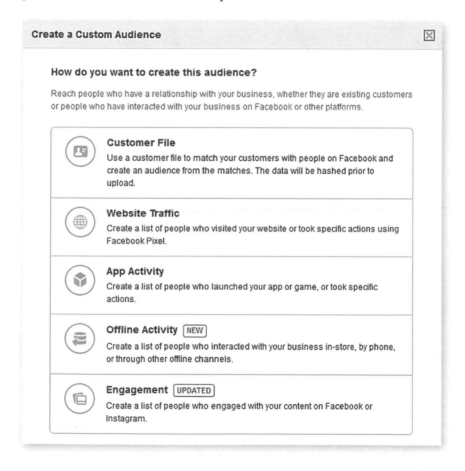

CUSTOMER FILE: Already discussed in chapter 5. This allows you to upload the emails and phone numbers of clients to create an initial audience.

WEBSITE TRAFFIC: Facebook maintains detailed information regarding which of its users actually clicked on the ads that you've placed. So while your ad might have gone out to ten thousand people in the first couple of days, what if only a hundred people clicked or commented on your ad? Obviously, something about the subject matter of the ad or your services compelled some people to stop scrolling through their feed and click or comment on the ad. You don't want to lose those people. You can set up whatever retargeting parameters you want. If you want to retarget only those who visited your website or your landing page, you can do that. If you want to send your ads only to those who spent a certain amount of time on your site or who visited within a certain period of time, you can do that as well. All this is possible thanks to the power of Facebook's pixel.

The key is to show those people an ad a second time, because they've already shown interest. So return the favor by reminding them that you're out there and might be the right law firm for them.

APP ACTIVITY: Usually not pertinent for lawyers. This option helps advertisers zero in on people who have used a particular app or game.

OFFLINE ACTIVITY: Another option that usually isn't applicable to law firms. More often this is helpful for retailers who want to target specific people who have visited their brick-and-mortar locations.

ENGAGEMENT: This is an extremely important tool for lawyers and law firms who advertise on Facebook, as it allows you to retarget Facebook users who have interacted with your ads or individual action pages. For the majority of the advertising campaigns that we have created for our clients, we have used this engagement option as a key starting point for retargeting strategies and distilling down a large audience into a more concentrated pool of likely PNCs.

Once you select the **Engagement** option, you will see a new menu of retargeting options, which should include the following. Let's break down each tool, one at a time.

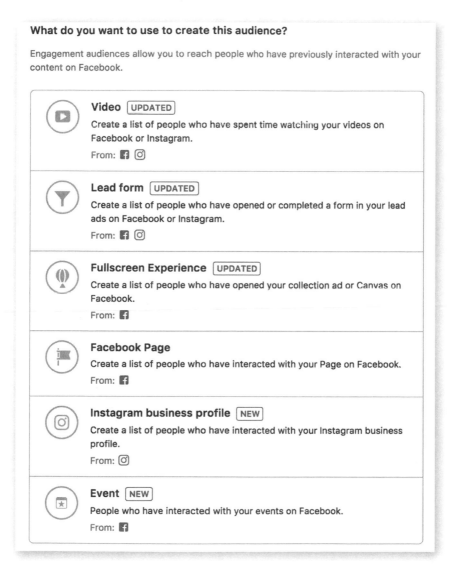

What do you want to use to create this audience?

Engagement audiences allow you to reach people who have previously interacted with your content on Facebook.

Video UPDATED
Create a list of people who have spent time watching your videos on Facebook or Instagram.
From:

Lead form UPDATED
Create a list of people who have opened or completed a form in your lead ads on Facebook or Instagram.
From:

Fullscreen Experience UPDATED
Create a list of people who have opened your collection ad or Canvas on Facebook.
From:

Facebook Page
Create a list of people who have interacted with your Page on Facebook.
From:

Instagram business profile NEW
Create a list of people who have interacted with your Instagram business profile.
From:

Event NEW
People who have interacted with your events on Facebook.
From:

VIDEO: If you've created a video-based advertisement or uploaded a video to your individual action page, this is a very powerful tool. Here's another classic example of just how much customization

Facebook allows. Click the engagement box and Facebook will ask you for more details on whom you want to target. Do you want to send ads to people who have watched three seconds of your ad (i.e., pretty much anyone who started the video) or ten seconds of your ad, or do you prefer to think in percentages? Perhaps Facebook users who watched 25 percent, 50 percent, 75 percent, or 95 percent of your video?

You can also set timeline parameters. Do you want to target anyone who visited in the last year or simply those who visited in the last couple of weeks or days? The parameters are entirely up to you. Simply select your targeting parameters, click on the **Choose Video** option to select which video you will be focusing on, and name your audience. Facebook will do the rest.

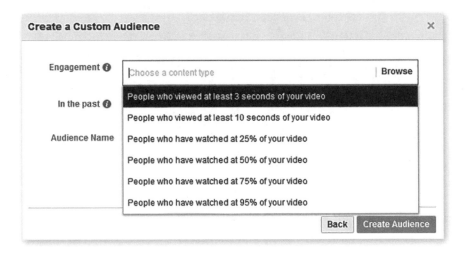

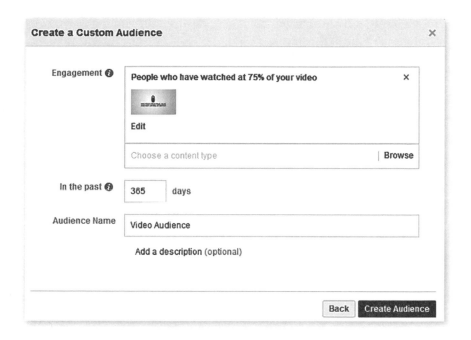

After you finish this part of the process, Facebook will take some time to create a new audience. Eventually, you will encounter an additional prompt. You can expand your audience or create an ad using the audience you just created. The choice is yours.

LEAD FORM: This is another extremely helpful tool. Clicking this option will empower Facebook to create an audience of people who have either visited the form on the front of your website landing page or actually filled out a form. We will discuss the importance of creating effective landing pages and forms in chapter 8. What's critical to realize is that anyone who took the time to click the "Learn More" button on your ad or clicked on a post in your individual action page likely has some degree of interest in your services. By creating an audience of people who took these steps, you can direct your ads to these interested parties. Sometimes, the difference between a lead and a potential new client is simply the product of showing those interested parties an ad a second time.

Once again, completing this form is very self-explanatory. From the drop-down menu, you can tell Facebook to retarget anyone who (a) opened the form, (b) opened the form but didn't submit it, or (c) filled out the form. You select the time interval you want Facebook to use, name your audience, and click away.

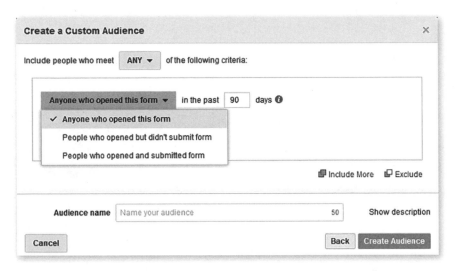

FULL SCREEN EXPERIENCE: We rarely use this retargeting strategy. It's for something called a Canvas Ad, which is Facebook parlance for your website. Facebook can track who is coming to your site, but thanks to the power of your pixel, which already monitors this information, it's a bit obsolete.

FACEBOOK PAGE: This is another good one. This tool enables Facebook to create a list of people who interacted with your individual action page. After you click this option, note the new menu of options that is presented to you.

You can tell Facebook to create an audience of people who visited your page, engaged with a post or ad, clicked a call-to-action button, sent you a message, or saved a page or post. This is an example of how Facebook allows you to cast a large net or employ a more targeted approach. Normally, we recommend that our clients focus on Facebook users who have actually engaged with a post or ad, which means they clicked the link, "liked" it, shared it, or commented on it.

In some cases, you may want to zoom in a bit more, perhaps only on those who showed a deeper interest and clicked the call-to-action or "Learn More" button, which narrows your search even more.

Whatever you choose, just remember that it can be extremely helpful to create a lookalike audience that resembles this group. It's one thing to retarget those who have already interacted with an ad or post and it's another thing entirely to allow Facebook to go trawling through its database for people who have yet to even see your ad or know that your individual action page exists and then direct your ads to them.

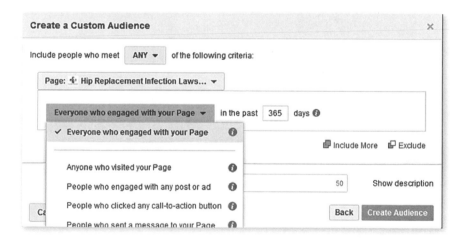

INSTAGRAM BUSINESS PROFILE: Once again, this is an option rarely used by lawyers. In the future, law firms may be heavy users of Instagram, but for the time being they are not.

EVENT: We always recommend our clients not overlook this last option. If you've sent out invitations for a particular event, such as a talk or a town hall meeting, through Facebook, the platform will catalog everyone you sent the invite to as well as those who responded that they were interested or RSVPd that they were going. Targeting your next batch of ads to people who showed interest and couldn't come or who actually attended the event can be a reminder that your firm is ready and waiting to help them should they be interested in taking legal action.

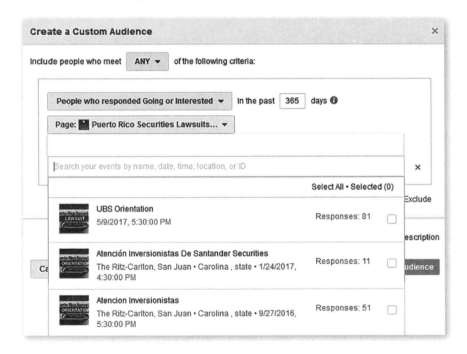

LOOKALIKE TARGETING SUCCESS: THE LANDING PAGE SECRET

Remember that line of secret code—the all-knowing pixel spy—that you installed on your website? Since you placed that Facebook pixel, it has been gathering information about who visited your site. Facebook can look for patterns between all those people and then create a lookalike audience of Facebook users who fit those patterns. In many cases, the most effective approach is to have Facebook create a lookalike audience from those who filled out a form on your site, what we call **conversions**. Now your additional set of ads will instantly go to people who are similar to those who have already filled out a form.

How to do it: The key is to generate a lookalike audience of people who have visited your landing page or people who have visited a specific page on your website. First we need to create the audience by returning to our Ads Manager page. Here is the string to follow:

Audiences → Create Audience → Custom Audience → Website Traffic (for all traffic) or **Audiences → Create Audience → Custom Audience → Website Traffic → People who visit specific web pages**.

Once you lock your sights in place, your audience will continue to change and evolve as more people are pulled to your website due to your advertising efforts.

Now, to generate a lookalike audience of your basic audience, select the audience by clicking the box next to it and click

Action and select **Lookalike Audience**. When you come to the **Lookalike Audience** page, you need to provide a location (likely the United States) and then select the **Advanced** option. You will see **Number of Audiences** with a drop-down menu. You want to create three lookalike audiences—those being 1 percent of all Facebook, 1 to 2 percent of all Facebook, and 3 to 5 percent of all Facebook. So the 1 percent of all lookalikes will be the most targeted, but the other two audiences will still get you people who are similar.

Let's return for a moment to our Invokana case. We've already shown how the Audience Insights tool allows a firm to look for hidden similarities within an audience (i.e., many amputees shop at certain stores for clothing or equipment). Now consider the power of performing the above advertising strategies simply for people who suffered from kidney complications and were on the drug.

Once we established an initial audience of Invokana users, we created lookalike audiences based on who interacted with our ads as well as who signed up to be a new client on our firms' websites. As a result of these strategies, we were able to provide a group of law firms with more than a thousand names of people who may have suffered from kidney failure as a result of Invokana.

Think about it like fishing. When you're on Facebook, you began with a vast, inefficient net, hoping to catch random fish in a vast ocean. But over time, Facebook has told you which rivers, ponds, and streams are most likely to house the fish that you really want to catch. Leverage the platform correctly and all of a sudden you find yourself pulling up tons of quality fish at a far more rapid clip, spending half the time and buying a fraction of the costly bait you would have needed otherwise.

The old maxim holds true, even in the digital realm: "Give a man a fish and you feed him for a day. Teach him how to fish and you feed him for a lifetime."

REPEAT AFTER ME: THE HIDDEN POWER OF REPETITIVE FACEBOOK ADVERTISING

I also encourage you not to underestimate the importance of repetition—especially the importance of showing promising audiences the same ads more than once. Although this is a rough estimate, I'd wager that 95 percent of the people who casually visit your firm's website will not sign a new client form or pick up the phone and call you until they've taken the time to mull things over.

Like it or not, this is human nature. Whenever we have a big decision to make—whether it's buying a new car or something as vital as choosing the right surgeon to perform a medical procedure—we fret about making a bad decision.

Some decisions we don't worry about at all. Undecided about which potato chips to bring to a party? Not a problem. You spend a minute in the snack aisle scanning all the options and you're done. But the higher the perceived value of the decision—i.e., the more expensive and important the decision—the more time we take to get it right.

Think about purchasing a new car. Most people visit a showroom. They test drive a car or two. They compare features and price. Surf the web a bit more. Ask friends. And then revisit their options to actually make a decision.

Most people take the same approach when hiring a lawyer. They want to look around. They want to vet you. They don't want to be fleeced, so they scrutinize things like image and text choice and how easy it is to navigate your site. And then what do people do? They take a break.

Legal shoppers tell their spouses that they want to sleep on things, and then they wind up sleeping on that decision for days or weeks—which is why you need to continually retarget your audiences. To convince undecided users to become clients, you want your ad to show up on their Facebook feed at the point when they realize time is ticking away and they need to make a decision.

I could write a whole separate book about the psychology of Facebook users. People trust Facebook because they feel ownership over their feeds. If you had to buy a home filled with other people's furniture and color schemes or a different home for the same price that you could design yourself, which would you choose?

Lesson: people are more invested in things they feel ownership over.

When users see a lawyer's face show up on Facebook, most assume that Facebook is recommending that lawyer. (Even though the platform doesn't actually recommend anyone.) I can't tell you how many people have told me, "Well, I saw the firm on my Facebook feed, so it must be a good and trustworthy firm."

By showing motivated potential clients your ad more than once, you are improving the odds that they will actually sign on with you as opposed to another website or firm they might have visited.

Thus, every time the quality of your audience improves via retargeting and the creation of a lookalike audience, the price it costs to gain a potential new client drops. Facebook learns. It distills. And then it delivers.

Let me give you an example of how your advertising costs actually go down over time. According to recent internal estimates that we've run, our ad campaigns usually cost about 1 to 3 cents per impression. If you optimize your audience, you are paying roughly $10 to $30 for a thousand people to see your ad.

Being able to ensure that $10 gets your ad to a thousand interested individuals is an achievement in itself, but consider our average conversion rates (i.e., the average cost for our Facebook ads to actually deliver a potential new client, or PNC). Our average conversion cost is $35 per PNC. Compared to other advertising platforms—whether it's TV, radio, or billboards—this is an astounding number.

Let me put it to you a different way: If someone told you that for every $35 check you wrote they could get you a PNC, would you take it?

If you've followed the audience-generating techniques outlined in this book, you should start to see real solid leads (i.e., people who have clicked on your ads, gone to your website landing page, and then followed it to your website, where they filled out a new client form) within the first $100 of advertising spend. But as you continue to refine your audience and generate lookalike audiences using these strategies, you will begin to come closer and closer to our magic number of $35 per PNC, which is a staggering bargain compared to the conversion averages offered just about anywhere else.

CHAPTER 8

Building a Digital Mousetrap: Blueprints for Building a Better Landing Page

AS WE'VE DEMONSTRATED, Facebook advertising campaigns are the most efficient lead generators that money can buy. They can sweep across the vast expanse of Facebook users—whether in local markets or across the country—and find the quality needles in the proverbial haystack.

The platform's tools can help you identify individuals who are likely to be interested in your legal services and then slip ads into their news feeds, generating a valuable bank of potential new clients. But as every lawyer knows all too well, there's a vast difference between generating leads and landing actual clients.

In order to convert leads into clients, firms need to ensure that whenever a Facebook user clicks on one of their ads or a post, they will be directed to an outside website that does two things: (1) filter out those who don't qualify as a client, and (2) encourage visitors to provide their contact information for a follow-up call.

We refer to these all-important websites—which are built outside of Facebook's framework—as **landing pages**.

Over the years, we've conducted comprehensive studies exploring what kinds of landing pages boost conversion rates and which do not—and built a comprehensive set of blueprints for building an effective landing page.

First, a few notes on simple approaches that won't generate as many conversions as you might expect.

DON'T RELY ON CALLBACK NUMBERS ALONE

Although it's important for all of your Facebook ads—as well as some posts on your individual action pages—to include your phone number, don't assume that simply posting a callback number is enough to generate a call.

While it is true that PNCs who are extremely motivated to retain a lawyer will have no problem dialing you, the vast majority of PNCs—roughly 90 percent according to our research—still hesitate to contact a law firm by phone.

Providing a means for motivated PNCs to talk to someone is extremely important, but don't lull yourself into believing that your phone number alone is enough to seal the deal. To convert a higher percentage of PNCs, you need to do much more.

DON'T ASK FOR PERSONAL INFO UPFRONT

We've worked with law firms that immediately asked for contact information on their landing pages, which was better than merely leaving a phone number but definitely not the most successful formula. Although these information requests were fairly innocuous—name, address, phone numbers, and email—PNCs still showed a reticence to provide their personal information without greater context. There's still a belief, perhaps not entirely unfounded, that if a lawyer is asking too many personal questions too quickly, he or she may be harboring an ulterior motive.

FORM PRECEDES FUNCTION:
FORMS THAT GENERATE CONVERSIONS

We've found that the most effective landing pages greet visitors with a series of simple questions that relate to a given lawsuit or particular practice strength. Although the remainder of your landing page includes important information, which we will describe later in the chapter, your primary focus should be on building an effective **opening form**.

Take, for instance, a form we developed for a firm searching for NFL players who suffered concussions. The first thing that visitors to this landing page encountered was a box containing two simple questions. In order to "qualify" and move on to the next screen, they had to answer these questions "correctly."

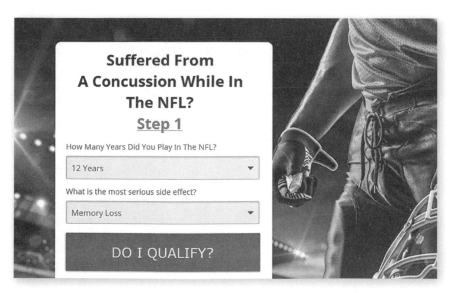

Think for a moment about that critical term "qualify." Marketers use it all the time, whether for retail sales pitches ("rewards card" members qualify for a special discount or sale) or showcase special perks (those who amass a hundred thousand frequent-flyer miles qualify for access to a special airport lounge).

In our experience, telling PNCs that only a select number of respondents will "qualify" is a great motivator. Most people are immediately interested in seeing if they will make the cut. It's human nature to wonder what's on the other side of a barricade. And because we know that your Facebook leads already have some interest in hiring a lawyer, they tend to answer questions to find out what comes next.

The key is to ensure that this initial form is simple and intuitive for visitors yet provides your firm enough basic information to decide whether the lead is worthy of adding to your client list.

What you're really trying to do with your opening form is build a smooth glide path that will encourage people to provide you their personal contact information later in the process. Every step that a PNC takes—i.e., every question they answer—emboldens them to continue forward and answer more questions.

Think of each step as a micro-commitment, which ultimately leads to the ultimate goal of contacting them in person and signing them up as clients.

What you don't want to do is overload people with too many questions or make your queries too difficult to answer. Limit this opening page to anywhere from two to five questions maximum. Be direct and simple. We recommend creating some opening questions that can weed out non-clients. If you're working on a lawsuit, think about some variables that will disqualify someone from the suit.

Sometimes this involves time limits (when someone took a medication); other times it involves the severity of an injury or side effect (developing sinus problems is far different than developing emphysema); and still other times you might have to ask whether the severity of their injury falls within the parameters of the suit.

After all, you don't want to spend precious time and energy on leads who will never qualify as clients. At the same time, you want those who might qualify to feel like they've accomplished something and made it to the "next level."

In the case of our opening form for the concussion lawsuit, we asked PNCs how many years they played in the NFL—from one year to fifteen-plus years. Zero years wasn't an option. If they didn't play in the NFL, they didn't qualify. Period.

Consider, however, the importance of question two, which asked visitors to select their most serious side effect from a list of prescribed options. This was important information for our clients, as different injuries paid out different settlements. Memory loss or depression might earn an ex-NFL player some money, but the advent of Parkinson's disease or serious brain injury would likely generate a larger sum.

After filling in these answers, former NFL players had to click on a big red button that read "Do I Qualify?" PNCs then saw a **processing screen**. It processed their answers quickly, like the bar on a website loading at broadband speed, but it reinforced the notion that our client had assessed their answers and provided them an opportunity to move on.

The second page of our NFL landing page opened with the word "Congratulations!" in large green letters, followed by a confirmation that they'd made the cut. The text read: *Based on your answers we believe you have a claim! Please fill out the contact form for a free consultation with our law firm to start your case.*

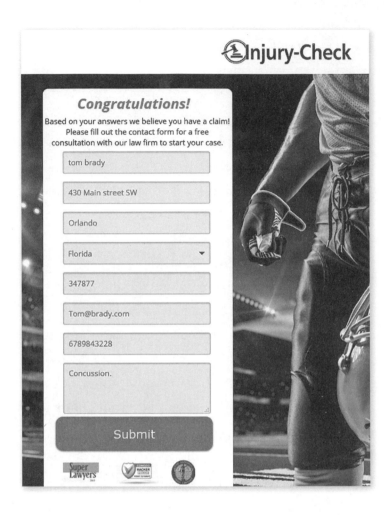

Never underestimate the importance of validating a PNC's experience or reminding the respondent that their injuries may translate into a financial settlement of some kind. People feel a psychological boost when they are told they have been wronged or payouts may be in their future—and thus they feel incentivized to continue answering more questions.

Law firms need to ensure this last list of questions is very direct and intuitive. Create a simple **contact information form**: address, email, telephone number, and a box that asks PNCs to add any additional information.

What you're doing, in essence, is building a digital mousetrap. You want to get people to the cheese (the contact information page), but you need to lay down some bread crumbs to get them there. You want to make them give a little to potentially get a lot more in return.

The last step? Make them feel like they actually reached the cheese. Create a final page that validates their time and informs them that they will be receiving a phone call from you or one of your representatives. Often it's important, as we did with the NFL case, to ask respondents not to contact other law firms, but what is absolutely critical is that you reaffirm the trust you've already established with your PNC.

In our NFL campaign, we initiated a discussion about price, explaining that there were no upfront charges and no financial obligations, and that their attorney would only get paid if he or she won the case.

YOU'RE ALL SET!

You will receive an important phone call from our legal intake team within the hour. Please do not contact another law firm before we have the opportunity to speak with you. You may not recognize the phone number but please answer our call so we can help you.

There is NO charge to you for exploring your legal options and absolutely no financial obligations! There is no upfront charge to you at all and your attorney will only get paid if he or she wins your case! You have nothing to lose and so much to gain.

Injury-Check

After meticulously testing a number of different approaches, there's little doubt that these landing pages work effectively, especially when it comes to conversion rates. When law firms merely left their phone number, only .2 percent of all potential leads (i.e., the most motivated PNCs) voluntarily contacted the firm. A standard form, which asked for PNCs to immediately offer their contact information, improved the numbers a bit, but only resulted in a 1 percent conversion rate.

The template we provided above—with its qualifying questionnaire as the lead—yielded a 3 to 5 percent conversion rate, which translates to a 300 to 500 percent increase over other landing page designs. When you convert that to actual client numbers, it's a pretty impressive leap, especially when you consider just how many leads a good Facebook campaign can attract.

With the right landing page, you can count on three to five solid conversions for every hundred visits. Start multiplying those numbers by factors of ten and you find yourself with an impressive stable of potential new clients.

BENEATH THE SKIN: THE ARCHITECTURE OF A LANDING PAGE

When it comes to building a successful landing page, it's critical to remember that 84 percent of Facebook clicks come from mobile devices. When a PNC clicks an ad on their smartphone, you need to make sure that they're greeted by the opening form that we outlined above—and nothing else. You want that form to fill up the entirety of their screen so that they're motivated to start answering questions and move on to the next screen, where they can input their contact information.

That being said, you can't assume that everyone will immediately jump in and start answering your questions. Facebook users are notorious for scrolling down and exploring website pages. They like to see what else is on a given site, so it's vital to add additional content below the form as well.

All of this additional information should be focused on reinforcing trust and encouraging people to scroll back up to your opening form and fill it out. Here's some advice on how to populate the rest of your landing page and why each addition is important.

Let's stay for a moment with the landing page we created for the NFL concussion lawsuit and scroll down to reveal what lies beneath the opening form.

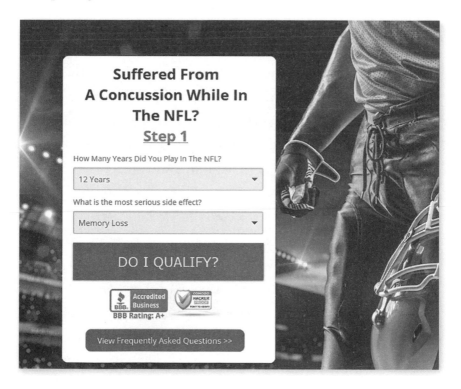

DO A PHOTO WRAP

Although most visitors will come to your landing page from a smartphone, there will always be a certain percentage of people who arrive via a desktop computer. The screen size on a desktop is much larger than a smartphone, so you need to place your opening form in front of the background image. You don't want your landing page to look cheap or cobbled together, which will make PNCs hesitate. So use a high-res image that's related to your firm's practice or the lawsuit in question and lay it down as a background pic. In this case, we used an image of a generic football player standing in the middle of a crowded stadium. The photo reinforced to PNCs that they had indeed come to the right place, while adding color to what can often be a rather bare, vanilla-looking form.

PLACE TRUST ICONS

You will note that there are two circular images below the "Do I Qualify?" button. We call these **trust icons**. They were first developed many years ago for e-commerce websites as a means to reassure people that a website was safe and secure. As a lawyer, you want to offer PNCs that same peace of mind. In this case, we used a Comodo HackerProof sticker to prove the site was safe, but there are plenty of other companies that offer web security services as well.

We also displayed a Better Business Bureau rating. Everyone is familiar with the BBB, which is why it's a reliable icon to use. But don't be afraid to show off whatever legal awards and honors that your law firm has won over the years. Think of this space as a trophy case. Even if a visitor doesn't know what a particular award means, the inclusion of an award on your landing page builds trust and confidence.

CONSIDER A SHORTCUT

In some cases, particularly with complex lawsuits, it's helpful to remind people what led them to your landing page in the first place. Obviously the content of your ad or individual action page was trust-worthy enough to entice a PNC to click it, so consider summarizing the bullet points of the lawsuit or your practice a second time on your landing page.

In this case, we created a button labeled "View Frequently Asked Questions," which sent people to the bottom of our landing page. FAQs for every case or lawsuit will be different, but by reiterating some key points, you reinforce your knowledge and dispel doubts.

Frequently Asked Questions

Question: I only played for a season before my injury – is that enough to qualify for this program?

Answer: YES. If you played at least a half season you meet the requirement.

Question: Can I participate even if I didn't play for the NFL?

Answer: YES. Players who played for the World League and in NFL Europe are also able to participate in this program.

Question: I wasn't an active player – is there still a way I can qualify?

Answer: YES. If you were on the practice, development, or taxi squad, you can participate, even if you didn't have an eligible season.

Question: I wasn't originally diagnosed with a concussions, but my doctor says that's what I had – do my injuries qualify?

Answer: YES. In the past, concussions weren't diagnosed and documented as they are now, but if you were injured, you may still qualify.

Question: I was injured, but I don't currently have a qualifying diagnosis, would I still be eligible?

Answer: YES. We can refer you to a physician who specializes in sports injuries and concussions to get you and accurate diagnosis.

Question: I have a series of symptoms including memory loss, trouble speaking, reading and writing, and difficulty completing tasks – can I find out if these symptoms are a result of my injury and not another condition such as Alzheimer's?

Answer: YES. We work with professional physicians who can examine you and your history to identify the cause of your current health condition.

EMPATHIZE OR EXCITE

Directly below your opening form and trust icons, you'll want to write a short headline and summarize the case or lawsuit. Think of this as a fact box that motivates people to go back to your opening form and fill it out. Sometimes you want to motivate with empathy—other times with the prospect of a large payout. If you can do both in just a few paragraphs, that's even better.

In the case of the NFL lawsuit, we reiterated that the lawsuit was open to anyone who played in the NFL. We bolded the fact that players could receive up to $5 million and reminded PNCs that the fund had already been established by the NFL, as well as the fact that they didn't have to be currently suffering from symptoms to qualify.

Then we placed an NFL logo on the screen—as we didn't want a stark white page—and reposted the firm's phone number, along with a reminder that visitors could call twenty-four hours a day, seven days a week.

Are You A Retired NFL Player?

If you played for the NFL you may be entitled to substantial compensation: **up to $5 million** for the most serious injuries. This money has been made available through a settlement fund established because of the serious risks caused by repetitive concussions and the NFL's prior knowledge of these risks.

You can participate in the NFL concussion settlement even if you are not suffering from memory loss or other concussion symptoms right now.

This was followed by a short paragraph reminding PNCs that we were on their side. It summarized the history of concussions in the National Football League and leaned on keywords that might resonate with PNCs, including phrases like "negligence," "head trauma," and "breached their duty."

Why Do **You Need** a Lawyer?

The registration and subsequent follow-ups involved with filing an NFL concussion settlement claim is very complicated.

If you do not file your claim properly you may lose your right to ever receive financial compensation from the NFL, even if you develop concussion symptoms in the future. It is also critical that you receive neurological testing from a quality, independent doctor. This means a doctor who is not working for the NFL. There is a **limited amount of time** to get this independent testing before new participants in this settlement will have to undergo testing by NFL-approved doctors.

Former Players Have Held the **NFL Accountable**

In 2011, a group of retired professional football players filed personal injury lawsuits against the NFL and related entities, alleging negligence. This meant that the organizations had breached their duty of care in failing to take reasonable action to protect players from the long-term harm of playing football. For many years, scientific findings repeatedly established that individuals who sustain repeated head trauma, such as concussions, are at an increased risk of permanent brain trauma. Studies have found that former NFL players have suffered chronic brain injuries from playing football, including:

- Parkinson's syndrome
- Dementia
- Memory loss
- Cognitive defects
- Changes in mood and personality
- Mental illnesses

FINAL FACTS: At the close of your landing page, it's often helpful to briefly explain what work your firm will perform on behalf of their clients and discuss any time limits or other actions that PNCs might need to take to qualify. In this case, our landing page reminded visitors that at some point they would have to be tested for brain injuries and that those tests had to be completed soon.

It's also important to close every landing page with standard terms of service language, which outlines privacy policies and specific terms of use. This is standard language that every law firm should have at their disposal, but one that's necessary to include on every landing page.

With this framework in place, the odds that PNCs will take the time to provide you with their contact information increase exponentially. All of your efforts to build effective ads, generate dialog on your individual action pages, and build an audience of potential clients ultimately funnels through this all-important landing page. This leaves only a single important step left: the equally important task of contacting PNCs and motivating them to sign a contract and become a client of your firm, which is the subject of our next chapter.

CHAPTER 9:

Speed to Lead: Converting Leads into Clients

THE FINAL STEP of a successful advertising campaign—the act of acquiring contact information and then reaching out to PNCs to formally sign an agreement—is dependent on both speed and patience in equal measures.

Too many law firms mistakenly believe that once they get a PNC's contact information, they have the luxury of time. Nothing could be further from the truth. Once a lead comes into a law firm's inbox, it's essential to begin reaching out to people immediately—within no more than five to ten minutes. X Social Media has developed a "Speed to Lead" product that automatically calls the law firm and then the client and connects the two within ten seconds of an online form being filled out. This is just one way we try and improve lead conversions for our clients.

Sound extreme? It isn't. Most people, including motivated potential clients, have very short attention spans as well as divided loyalties. You need to strike while the iron is hot and they're still actively thinking about the form they just filled out on your landing page.

Remember, thanks to your ads and your individual action pages, you've planted a seed in their mind that they have a case or that they need a lawyer. If you take too long to reconnect with a PNC, they will begin researching other law firms or clicking on other Facebook ads, which will allow another lawyer to sweep in and poach your client.

Initially, you have an advantage in that you've helped educate them and earned their trust via Facebook. Let's say you built a campaign around a lawsuit involving a drug that caused serious and undocumented side effects. You have already taken the time to inform them that there is a correlation between a drug they have taken and a particular injury they are experiencing.

That's incredibly important social capital. They don't know the hundreds of other law firms that could take their case, but they feel like they know and trust *you*.

Don't squander that trust by handing off their contact information to an overworked lawyer who doesn't have the time or patience to close a contract. Time is too precious for most lawyers to immediately drop what they're doing to follow up on a lead.

What you need instead is a dedicated intake representative—or better yet, a group of intake representatives—specifically trained to convert leads into clients. If you have the capital, it's often advantageous to hire an outside call center to handle all callback tasks, as most vendors are equipped to return calls after five or six o'clock or on weekends, when many PNCs fill out forms.

That being said, it can be more cost-effective to keep things in-house, provided you develop the right intake system, hire the right people, and provide the right training. An outline of what works and what doesn't work follows.

TRY A LITTLE TLC

Whether you hire an outside call center or keep your conversion team in-house, it's essential that you tailor your process to meet the needs of your potential clients, most of whom will require more attention and patience than your everyday consumer. Here's a checklist of best practices that have generated success for our law firm clients across the country.

SEND A TEXT FIRST

Even if a PNC has just filled out a form, many people are wary of answering a call from a number they don't recognize. Some people are trying to avoid bill collectors; others don't want to deal with yet another spam call. And if you're dealing with an elderly population, they might be wary about talking to anyone they don't know.

To ease these fears, immediately text anyone who filled out a contact form. The text should include a short note thanking them for filling out your form, reminding them of the name of your firm, and informing them that they will be receiving a call. Then list the phone number that your team members will be calling from.

Email communications don't work as well, because so many automatically get swept into junk folders, but texts typically go directly to an individual's phone and can arrive in real time, often mere minutes after a PNC filled out a form.

GO SLOW, LISTEN, AND EMPATHIZE

Here is where the dichotomy between speed and patience comes to the forefront. Even though you may need to send out a text and call back PNCs as quickly as possible, it's absolutely vital that your representatives not rush through these calls.

This is not an instance where you want to hire young employees who are more concerned with riffling through a hundred calls an hour than taking the time to make a human connection with the person on the other end of the line.

The vast majority of PNCs want to talk about their problems or injuries. They want someone to listen to their story and validate their pain, so make sure to hire employees who are personable and capable of showing genuine compassion. Don't allow them to multitask. Discourage them from interjecting too forcefully. And prevent them from rushing directly into their questions.

A large swath of the population still harbors suspicions that lawyers are more concerned about money than justice. Don't feed into that stereotype. Make sure your people listen intently to the voices on the phone so that PNCs feel their pain is registering with the operator and the firm itself. If you make them feel like a number in a queue, they'll assume you aren't a good fit and look for a more compassionate firm.

ESTABLISH STRICT ELIGIBILITY CRITERIA

Once a rapport has been established, ensure that your callback representative has a clear list of questions that will determine if the PNC is a worthy client and aligns with the lawsuit at hand. It's often important to repeat some of the qualifying questions that you listed on your landing page.

After all, the PNC doesn't know which questions allowed them to qualify, so gently probe to ensure the lead didn't just tell you what they assumed you wanted to hear.

In the case of a lawsuit involving side effects from a medication, ask what drugs they are—or were—taking and when they started taking them. Ask PNCs to describe their injuries and the side effects they are experiencing. Ask if they stopped taking the drugs, and if so, when? Ask if they had to go to the hospital for treatment.

The goal is to acquire the information you need without delving too deeply into sensitive issues that will break trust. Walk that line carefully and you'll have a committed client.

ASSIST INDIVIDUALS WITH THE CONTRACTS

If a PNC appears to be a good fit for the firm or a particular suit, gently transition into a discussion regarding contracts. Show your manners and say something like "Would you be comfortable if I sent you a contract that you can execute from email or smartphone?"

In some cases, especially with elderly PNCs, you might need to physically send a contract via the mail, but it's best to email them immediately so that you can guide them through any trouble spots while you have them on the phone.

In the case of a medical lawsuit, you will need to send multiple forms, including a HIPAA contract. Explain to the PNC why their medical records are needed to qualify for the lawsuit. Walk through every aspect of the contract and try to be as transparent as possible. PNCs will pick up on your openness and follow your lead.

Law firms that don't properly address this final part of the process will allow as many as 75 percent of future clients to slip through their fingers. Why? Because a crowded backlog of unreturned calls grows exponentially larger and more burdensome every day.

Let's say, for example, that you don't hire enough callback operators to touch base with every PNC who filled out a form. On day one, your team failed to reach out to ten people. The next day you receive roughly the same amount of leads, but you now need to make up for the ten people you didn't have time to contact the day before. Now, you have twenty leads that you haven't contacted, a number that keeps snowballing and puts you further behind the eight ball.

Intake and processing is so important, in fact, that we created our own online training program called Xintake—http://xintake.com/opus/—which provides online training and e-learning tutorials to help law firms build their own highly efficient and cost-effective intake systems.

It's a thirteen-week program, which is divided into eighteen easily digestible one-hour sessions. The first course (Making the Connection) details how to make a good first impression, how to build empathy, and how to foster trust. The second course (Processes and Protocols) outlines how to build quality questionnaires, improve accuracy, and glean the right responses. The third course (Six Sigma Intake Department) offers advice on time management skills, daily workload responsibilities, and how to eliminate bottlenecks.

In between each course, we provide practice scenarios that allow trainees to encounter common questions and issues, while also reinforcing what was learned in the tutorials. Our law firm clients have found that this program provides a rare opportunity to quickly scale their intake work and ensure that all of their hires are working according to the same philosophies and best practices, which in turn boosts conversion rates.

Those that have followed our plan have seen additional benefits as well, including a sharp uptick in referrals as well as shrinking advertising costs, because every converted client allows a firm to successfully narrow their targeting strategies on Facebook.

In the end, no matter if you use our program, perform your own training, or hire an outside firm, there's little doubt that the right intake structure and callback personnel can be the difference between average returns and substantial new additions to your client list.

CONCLUSION

One More Thing

I'VE WRITTEN THIS BOOK in the hope that lawyers across the country will experience the same kind of Facebook awakening as I did in the wake of the Gulf oil spill.

Had it not been for that devastating tragedy, I wouldn't have realized how quickly and efficiently Facebook can become a bridge between individuals in need of legal assistance and law firms that can ably act as their advocates.

I'm convinced that increased usage of Facebook's advertising platform by the legal industry is ultimately a win-win for both lawyers and everyday Americans. The easier it is for individuals across this country to gain access to legal services, the more opportunities they will have to redress wrongs, offset the cost of major medical bills, and experience justice under the law.

Facebook is an especially powerful tool for the disenfranchised and wounded among us who wish to fight against the world's rich and powerful Goliaths. This platform provides an avenue for negligence to come into the light—for individuals who have been bankrupted by medical bills, who lost their job through no fault of their own, or who were wronged to connect with someone who can represent their interests.

Facebook advertising campaigns are a means for lawyers to go where their clients currently reside and where they spend the majority of their time while online. It's a place where they can advertise their services in a cost-effective way. Momentum propels change. The more interest that is generated by potential clients, the more quickly law firms, both large and small, will be able to grow their client list and expand their services.

In this regard, Facebook is a great equalizer. The more clearly that small and medium-sized law firms understand how Facebook works and what exactly it can do, the more likely they are to launch campaigns that are as magnetic as those run by major law firms.

The days when lawyers were reliant exclusively on pricey TV, radio, and billboard ads are officially over. Facebook's suite of advertising tools allows enterprising lawyers and firms to spend a fraction of what they might have in the past while reaching a far more concentrated and targeted group of potential clients.

Using the strategies we have outlined in this book, you can narrow your sights to the potential clients that are best suited for your firm or the lawsuit you are pursuing, while expanding your client list in the most affordable way possible.

In the end, Facebook advertising allows firms to provide PNCs what they yearn for most of all: the luxury of convenience. You can come to them and build a presence in their private Facebook world. You are eliminating the need for PNCs to summon up the courage to call you. And you are building individual action pages—which are the closest thing to a virtual community that we currently have—on a platform that boasts billions of followers.

Don't underestimate the value of your individual action pages. They're like quality real estate: the more you invest in them, the better returns they'll produce. Once you establish a page, you can keep it up and running forever. No one will have to search Google to find you. Place a new post on that page and you're getting free advertising, which will appear in the feeds of clients, friends, and strangers alike.

Facebook is destined to become the de facto advertising platform of the legal industry, but it's not there yet. Jump on now and you'll be getting in on the ground floor, staking a position in a critical space before your competitors attempt to do the same. Facebook is, without doubt, the digital advertising platform of the moment.

But I would be remiss, in the spirit of Steve Jobs, if I didn't mention one more thing. If Facebook is the medium of the moment, then I consider **behavioral digital tracking** to be its successor—a paradigm-busting advance that will alter the world of legal advertising just as much, if not more, than Facebook is doing at the current moment.

Think of it as lookalike targeting 2.0.

Today, Facebook monitors the "likes," posts, and interests of everyone on its platform. It maps out where its users go inside its platform and the sites its users visit online. But imagine for a moment a system that allows your firm to track where everyone—whether they are logged onto Facebook or not—is going on the internet as they are surfing?

What if you could look for patterns in the way PNCs searched the web—i.e., their online behavior patterns—so that you could identify potential clients before they even knew they needed a lawyer?

What if you were filing a lawsuit involving the side effects of a particular drug and we could hand you information about a set of people who went to WebMD.com to look up the specific side effects of that same drug and then documented how a subset of those same people started visiting legal websites? What if you could, in the middle of that search, suddenly send them an ad that spoke directly to their health concerns and their legal needs?

If Facebook usage accounts for 20 percent of all web usage, what if we could provide leads for the other 80 percent of web traffic? Imagine slipping ads in front of all of these potential clients as they are in the midst of their search.

Facebook allows you to send ads to a large swatch of people in specific geographic areas—like those sitting in hospitals with leg injuries—but what if I told you that we are able to hand you leads whose leg injuries were caused by a particular drug? Imagine the money that you could save in your advertising budget. Think about the efficiencies you could gain, as well as the speed and precision with which you could attract clients.

This new frontier in legal advertising—our behavioral digital tracking initiative—is not the sort of thing that can be translated into a book, but it is precisely the kind of next-generation service that we are now offering our clients.

For more information and details regarding how behavioral tracking can improve your practice, visit https://www.xsocialmedia.com/.

But in the meantime, I hope this book—an unveiling of all the secrets of Facebook advertising—will do what it was intended to do: open your eyes to the possibility of this amazing advertising platform. Follow the advice outlined in this book and you will be able to dramatically improve the online presence of your firm and ultimately earn a plethora of new clients at a fraction of the price that it's costing your competitors.

Remember to "Build. Target. Enhance." An advertising renaissance is within your reach.

Sincerely,

Jacob Malherbe